Wild Goose big book of liturgies & resources 3: Bread of hope

Wild Goose big book of liturgies & resources 3: Bread of hope

wild goose
publications
www.**ionabooks**.com

Contributions copyright © the individual contributors
Compilation © The Iona Community

Published 2023 by
Wild Goose Publications
Suite 9, Fairfield
1048 Govan Road, Glasgow G51 4XS, Scotland
A division of Iona Community Trading CIC
Limited Company Reg. No. SC156678
www.ionabooks.com

ISBN 978-1-80432-305-2

Cover photo © Kranich17 via Pixabay

The publishers gratefully acknowledge the support of the Drummond Trust, 3 Pitt Terrace, Stirling FK8 2EY in producing this book.

All rights reserved. Apart from the circumstances described below relating to non-commercial use, no part of this publication may be reproduced in any form or by any means, including photocopying or any information storage or retrieval system, without written permission via PLSclear.com.

Non-commercial use: The material in this book may be used non-commercially for worship and group work without written permission from the publisher. If photocopies of small sections are made, please make full acknowledgement of the source, and report usage to the CLA or other copyright organisation.

The Iona Community has asserted its right in accordance with the Copyright, Designs and Patents Act, 1988, to be identified as the author of this work.

Overseas distribution
Australia: Willow Connection Pty Ltd, 1/13 Kell Mather Drive,
Lennox Head NSW 2478
New Zealand: Pleroma, Higginson Street, Otane 4170,
Central Hawkes Bay

Printed in the UK by Page Bros (Norwich) Ltd

Contents

Introduction   7

Prayers for evening time, *Janet Lees*   9

First love yourself: A reflection and resources for Valentine's Day, *Alex Clare-Young*   15

As we celebrate the love: Worship resources for weddings, *Simon Taylor*   23

From dust to Easter dawn: Worship resources for Ash Wednesday, *Rodney Aist*   31

The dust of life: An Ash Wednesday evening service, *Thom M Shuman*   37

When I hear your voice: Stories, prayers and actions for International Women's Day, *Janet Lees*   45

We shout out their names and honour their courage: A reflection and prayer for the UN International Day of Remembrance of the Victims of Slavery and the Transatlantic Slave Trade (25th March), *Iain and Isabel Whyte*   55

The silent stars howl in grief: A liturgy for Passion Sunday, *Thom M Shuman*   59

Like cloaks laid on the ground: A liturgy for Palm Sunday, *Thom M Shuman*   67

Remembering mothers: Resources for Mother's Day, *Tom Gordon*   75

Go out into the darkness: A tenebrae for Maundy Thursday evening, *Janet Lees*   83

On a hill: An outdoor service for Good Friday, *Bob Warwicker and Janet Lees*   91

Drink this cup: A meditation and reflection, *Stephen G Wright*   101

On the other side of this day: A reflection for Holy Saturday, *John Murning*   107

Let there be light: Resources for Easter Day, *Rodney Aist*   111

Easter morning at the Split Rock, *Jan Sutch Pickard*   119

A wake-up call: A hymn for the Earth, *Tom Gordon*   129

I and the Other are one: Worship resources for Pentecost, *Rodney Aist*   131

Wild Spirit: A prayer for Pentecost, *Sandra Sears*   137

I walk with my father today: Worship resources for Father's Day, *Tom Gordon*   141

Holy space: A liturgy for St Benedict's Day (11th July), *Janet Lees*   151

Living rough, living sheltered: A service of solidarity with rough sleepers,
Urzula Glienecke   157

Remember me: Resources for the United Nations International Day for the Eradication of Poverty (17th October), *John Harvey, Ian M Fraser and Kathy Galloway*   165

Stones and bread, mourning and joy: Resources for Trans Day of Remembrance (20th November), *Alex Clare-Young*   173

That further shore: A simple liturgy for remembering someone who has died,
Simon Taylor   181

Rest beside quiet waters: A reflection for caregivers who may feel wearied,
Elaine Gisbourne   191

Shining the Light of Christ into a world of conflict: A liturgy and resources for Remembrance Sunday, *Nancy Cocks*   195

Take three: An Advent or Christmas meditation on gifts and power,
Stephen G Wright   211

The light shines in the darkness: A service for Christmas Eve or for Christmas Day,
Nancy Cocks   217

About the contributors   228

Introduction

The first thing I noticed when editing this anthology was – again – how wide-ranging it is. The rich variety says a lot about the life-in-all-its-fullness engagement of members and friends of the Iona Community. And as always with the Community, this is worship which is contextual, with a strong justice and peace edge.

A few of the pieces were written during the Covid pandemic, but of course have meaning beyond that time.

The liturgies and resources here were originally published as single digital downloads by Wild Goose. The book is a follow-up to the four other Wild Goose Big Books.

I hope that this collection helps to feed your life and the life of the world. In the words of Thom M Shuman:

Nourish us with the Bread of hope,
    that we might go into
    the brokenness of our world;

fill us with the cup of grace,
    so the weary will discover us
    standing by their side;

fill us with the overflowing joy
of the good news,
    so we might sing forever
    of your heart's desire
    for justice and peace for all people.

(Thom M Shuman, from 'Like cloaks laid on the ground')

– Neil Paynter, Wild Goose Publications

Prayers for evening time

Janet Lees

Introduction:

This is a set of worship items that could be used by a small group: a family, a community ... It includes simple songs/chants, ways of remembering the Bible, psalms and prayers. It's like a patchwork: join it together as seems fitting, with silence and perhaps music of your choice. I wrote it during the Covid-19 pandemic of 2020.

You might like to begin by lighting some candles and with songs or chants.

Songs:

What shall we do when the sun goes down?
(Tune: 'Drunken sailor')

This first one is traditionally a rowdy song, but can be sung quietly if you prefer.

What shall we do when the sun goes down?
What shall we do when the sun goes down?
What shall we do when the sun goes down
and the day has ended?

Think of the one who's risen,
Think of the one who's risen,
Think of the one who's risen,
early in the morning.

Or:

Evening falling
(Tune: 'Bunessan/Morning has broken')

Evening falling, sun is now stalling,
last rays are touching earth, sea and sky.
Velvet night beckons, moon and stars reckon
that with night falling their time is nigh.

Time is now slowing, day it is going,
earth is unwinding, light is now gone.
God is still watching, embracing, touching,
keeping all safe and singing love's song.

Prayer and reflection:

There's a day behind
and a night ahead,
and I'm thankful for both …

My heart is here and my attention.
My mind is here and my thoughts.
My body is here and my emotions.

The day and the night are both alike to you, O God.

We spend some time now re-running the day in our thoughts and prayers:

the people we met,
the things we did,
the Bible as we remember it.

We may keep silence, draw or make some other response or speak out loud …

All the things I would have said,
all the things I should have said,
all the things I could have said,
all the things I never said,
still hang here like muffled bells,
waiting, ready to break the silence.
Christ, have mercy.

Somewhere in the world,
if not where you are right now,
people are struggling to breathe for many different reasons.
As we settle to rest
we breathe again and remember them …
Crucified Christ, visited with violence,

body torn, bleeding, dying,
you hung on for us,
each agonising breath its own torture:

may we hang on for and with each other,
naming the need to breathe as basic justice,
crying out for the earth's traumatised ones.
Only your love can make 'the new normal'
the place where difference flourishes.
Christ, have mercy.

Psalm snippets: recall (or read) any section or snippet of a Psalm and spend some time thinking, talking about it, for example:

From Psalm 4:

You made room for me when I was upset.
I will lie down and sleep in peace,
for only you, God,
make room for me to do so safely.

From Psalm 17:

Keep me safe from those who would hurt me:
protect me as the apple of your eye;
hide me safely under your wings.

Lord's Prayer (in whatever language or form you prefer):

Here's one. Note that I use the word 'kindom' rather than 'kingdom' to represent a gender-equal community.

Holy One, uniting earth and heaven,
nurturing us and all things,
bringing us together in your kindom:
may it happen here and everywhere.
Give us bread to eat today
and forgiveness for the way we cheat others of their bread,
as we forgive those who have stolen ours.

May we not take revenge,
and keep us safe from corruption,
as we try to pursue your kindom of equality, peace and justice,
giving you thanks and glory.
Amen

Nunc Dimittis: Luke 2:29–32

A version here:

Holy God, now let your weary servant go in peace.
Your promise to see the hope and love you have prepared for us
has been kept.
It is wonderful indeed.
Like a light:
glorious in every way to those who embrace your kindom.
Glory, glory, glory,
Creator, Son and Spirit,
Amen, Amen, Amen.

I see the evening sun go down.
I await the rising of the morning Son.
God grant a quiet night
and a peaceful end.

Blessing:

Take a candle and face your neighbour, and say this blessing all together:

The Blessing of the Creator, light you.
The Blessing of the Risen Son, light you.
The Blessing of the Light-giving Spirit, light you.
May the Holy Three give you light, love and peace
this night and forever.

Extinguish the candle.

First love yourself
A reflection and resources for Valentine's Day

Alex Clare-Young

Love who?

God is love. For many, the 14th of February is a day filled with love. Valentine's Day in its contemporary form, filled with greeting cards and romantic dates, can be a wonderful thing. On this day, every year, millions of people are reminded of the importance of love. At its best, Valentine's Day helps us to love each other. For those in happy, healthy relationships, the love that a partner shows on Valentine's Day can be a vital point of reconnection and a much-needed reminder to love ourselves.

At its worst, though, Valentine's Day highlights our differences, heightens injustice and feeds consumerism. It hides the harsh realities of life, normalises relationships, alienates single people and is, for many, filled with sharp words and painful punches. What worries me most about Valentine's Day at the moment, though, particularly as I am writing from lockdown – at a time where, in many places, community love has been worn thin and social justice has been all but forgotten – is the damage I fear it does to the concept of Christian love. I am afraid that this day holds paradigmatic power. The power to whisper a dangerous lie … One tiny mistruth that does all sorts of damage … The lie is this: *'Christian love is about one thing, and one thing only: the relationship between a man and a woman in marriage.'*

Don't panic, this reflection and resource do not focus exclusively on LGBTQ+ identities and justice, though they are an important part of my considerations. The homophobia and heteronormativity behind the lie are horrific. This lie, though, does damage beyond the LGBTQ+ community. This lie hides the truth of one of God's most important commandments: *'Love your neighbour as you love yourself.'* Or, in other words, *'Love that one person, or that one community, that the world has taught you to hate. Oh, by the way, that commandment is not as simple as it sounds, because first you must love yourself.'* Christian love, you see, is not just about one normative, monogamous, romantic relationship. It's bigger than that. We are called to love the other.

So, can we subvert Valentine's Day?

On the 14th of February 2013 streets in cities around the world were awash with pink. In more than 190 countries, women gathered to turn a day that is traditionally celebrated with pretty pink greeting cards into a powerful protest against gendered violence. In 2021, as gatherings have moved online,

One Billion Rising (www.onebillionrising.org) asked people around the world to drum, dance, make art, create poetry, sing, wail, speak ... To record an action which would express outrage about and bring an end to violence towards women and LGBTQ+ people. To '... *RISE to end capitalism, colonisation, racism, imperialism, climate catastrophe and war*'.[1] This is just one example of how ordinary people might come together, on a day that is lovely for a few, troubling to many and deeply damaging to some, and make a difference about things that matter.

Concerning love

One of the ways that the Iona Community expresses its love for the other, and for the earth on which we live, is by meeting together – in person and over the Internet – to talk and pray, to write and campaign about our 'common concerns'. These are areas in life where we have noticed injustice and believe that we can, and should, make a change. The second part of our Rule, you see, is to *'work for justice and peace, wholeness and reconciliation in our localities, society and the whole creation'*.[2] Our Common Concern Networks[3] are part of the way that we work together to keep this Rule. And I think that the concept of love, and the way in which we celebrate Valentine's Day, is relevant to the work of every one of them.

Our Common Concerns are:

The environment
Faith and spirituality
Israel/Palestine
Migration and refugees
Poverty and inequality
Reconciliation, peacemaking and disarmament
LGBTQ+
Challenging racism

On the high streets of the UK and, increasingly, over the Internet, millions of people spend more than they can afford on their loved ones for Valentine's Day. Worryingly, it's no longer just a card – the amount of money spent rises and rises every year.[4] This consumerism, alone, touches on many of our concerns. What is our Valentine's Day card and gift obsession doing to the environment? Our oceans are full of the plastic wrappers and unwanted novelty items that go straight into the bin ... How does the pressure to spend hurt those already living in poverty and inequality? What are the effects of the debt caused by consumerist culture? ... Our concern about faith and spirituality raises similar questions: how did this Saint Day turn into a secular holiday?

A more community-focused understanding of love on Valentine's Day might be a powerful campaigning tool in our work for justice in other areas of concern. Perhaps instead of a focus on our own homes, we might use this time to focus on the homes that have been cruelly torn apart by division, violence and war. Maybe we could consider those spending this Valentine's Day in leaky boats or trudging through hostile terrain in a desperate search for safety, or those waiting in fear at a wall or a barbed-wire fence.

I am the Moderator of the Iona Community's LGBTQ+ Common Concern Network, and a transmasculine person. The thing is, for me, as for many other LGBTQ+ people, Valentine's Day doesn't feel authentic. It makes us feel like outsiders. Many newly out LGBTQ+ people spend Valentine's Day alone, ostracised by people who they thought were friends and the churches who they thought loved them. When the 14th of February is a Sunday, many LGBTQ+ folk are forced to listen to sermons about the importance of marriage and family, heteronormative ideals that they hope for, but that are often held just out of reach. Many trans people spend Valentine's Day afraid and in pain, unable to fully love themselves because all that they see in the media and experience on the streets is hatred. Leelah Alcorn's suicide note included the heartbreaking words, *'I'm never going to have enough love ... People say "it gets better" but that isn't true in my case. It gets worse ... I get worse'*.[5] Like many trans people, Leelah didn't feel loved by anyone, which made it next to impossible for her to love herself.

You first

If you are feeling upset or guilty about some of the things that I have written about so far, that is okay. I believe that we need to take time to sit with our pain and our guilt and to consider how we might help to make things better. If you want to make a difference, please do check out the links at the end of this resource, to 'One Billion Rising', to my own website, and to the Iona Community's Common Concern Networks.

But, for now, let's set that guilt and pain to one side. Right back at the beginning of this reflection, I quoted Jesus' rule: *'Love your neighbour as you love yourself.'* When I was training for ministry, a very wise colleague reminded me that there is a second rule hidden within that rule. It isn't just about loving other people. It starts with loving ourselves. It even follows that it is entirely impossible to love your neighbour if you hate yourself!

Time and time again, I have heard, and read, words that castigate young people for being self-centred, attention-seeking or individualistic. I would like to suggest, though, that by taking time to curate our individuality and to care for ourselves properly, we are trying to follow the rule of loving others as we love ourselves. And that love is sorely needed. In the days of culture wars, social isolation and increasingly toxic political and media behaviour, we need to relearn the art of self-care. God calls us to love ourselves better, so that we might go out into the world and love others.

Colours of love

So how might you take some time to love yourself better, so that you might better love others? There are lots of ideas and resources out there. For me, personally, nothing beats a hot bath and a good book. Or, when I have some more energy, a long walk in the fresh air does me the world of good. For this resource, though, I am going to suggest some self-care through colour and creativity.

In 1978, Gilbert Baker designed the LGBTQ+ pride flag. Now, flags can be divisive and dangerous, but they can also be helpful and healing. In the case of LGBTQ+ people, flags have helped us to feel less isolated, and to recognise where we might find other people who share some of our identities and experiences, allies, support and safe spaces. The colours used in the original flag were not random. They had meanings, and those meanings are worth thinking about, whatever your identity. They are pink for the physicality of identities and relationships, red for life, orange for healing, yellow for sunlight, green for nature, turquoise for art, indigo for harmony, and violet for spirit. To help to tease out these colourful concepts a little more, and to think about their relevance to social justice, here's a poem:

Pink

Pink is touch and love and pleasure,
but who am I and how can I live without measure?

Red is life and breath and blood,
but often it's shed in the dirt and the mud.

Orange is healing, reconciliation, change,
so where are my allies and why isn't there more rage?

Yellow is light and light exposes power and fakes,
so, we spill out our words, but they just call us 'snowflakes'.

Green is nature, energy, transformation,
and why are we sleeping through capitalisation?

Turquoise is art and you know, 'winter is coming'.
Because if activists are 'snowflakes' and 'pansies' our rage should be
an avalanche of creativity,
a garland of lived experience and a garden of words
that speak truth to power –
this is our need.
This is the hour.

Indigo is harmony and reconciliation,
when kin love each other and heal every nation.

Violet is spirit, which is all that we need,
to sit down together and organise against greed,
One Billion Rising, one billion, an avalanche –
one action, a movement, one activist, a snowflake – Me.

Labyrinths

Labyrinths are an ancient symbol, tool and practice that help us to remember that life is a journey, and that encourage, inspire and enable us to stop on our journeys and take some time to reflect, meditate and pray. A labyrinth might look like a maze, but it's different for one simple reason: it isn't trying to catch you out! A labyrinth should be fairly easy to follow, allowing your mind to wander and wonder. You don't have to take the journey all at once either. Many pilgrims stop on their way through the labyrinth to pause and to ponder. And it isn't just about getting into the middle! The journey back out of the labyrinth, on which we can prepare ourselves to face and to serve in the world, is just as important.

Because many people can't access physical labyrinths, finger labyrinths are becoming increasingly popular. These are mini-labyrinths that you can follow with your eyes, or finger, or a computer mouse. The labyrinths that I have doodled for you can be used as finger labyrinths. Just follow the patterned line. You can download these from: https://www.ionabooks.com/cms/wp-content/uploads/2023/07/Labyrinths-A4.pdf

You might like to try some adult colouring using the black-and-white labyrinth. Go on a journey. Which colours do you need in your life today? Which colours say something about who you are? Can you use colours to help you to untangle your concerns, and to pray for the situations in which you would like to be a changemaker?

Finally, you might like to use the coloured labyrinth in prayerful or meditative reflection. As you follow the patterned path into the centre of the labyrinth, work on loving yourself. Who are you? Where is your journey taking you? What do you need and desire? And, as you follow the path back out, work on loving the other. Who are they? Where is their journey taking them? What do they need and desire? What needs to change so that all might be loved?

If these labyrinths don't take your fancy, or if you're up for a further creative challenge, why not try drawing your own? There are lots of simple instructions and beautiful examples available online.

Notes and resources:

1. From the V Day website: https://vspot.vday.org/vday/events/58462. Also see: www.onebillionrising.org/about/campaign

2. The Rule of the Iona Community: https://iona.org.uk/about/our-community/our-rule/

3. Common Concern Networks of the Iona Community: https://iona.org.uk/our-resources/common-concerns/

4. https://www.finder.com/uk/valentines-day-statistics

5. https://amp.theguardian.com/world/2015/jan/05/sp-leelah-alcorn-transgender-teen-suicide-conversion-therapy

6. Beyond Binaries: https://alexclareyoung.co.uk/

As we celebrate the love
Worship resources for weddings

Simon Taylor

An alternative opening prayer for a wedding

God of love and life,
you have journeyed with us to bring us to this new beginning.
With the ebb and flow of the tide, day and night have passed,
yet you have been always present,
often in unexpected places and ways.

We thank you for those lives that have shaped us and guided us,
for the shared experiences that have deepened love and built trust.
We praise you that our lives are a thing of beauty fashioned by your hand,
and today ask that this joining together of two friends
will be a moment of celebration
giving way to a lifetime of joyful companionship.

We confess that we can quickly become cynical and unkind,
our joy diminished as the anxieties of life break in.
So help us, Lord, to be always open to you,
that we might be surprised by your constant presence,
ever touched by your gracious friendship
and filled with the peace your nearness gives.
Warm us with the fire of your compassion,
that we might know that we are loved
and are called to love without condition.

May your kindness and light fill this day,
as words of love and commitment are shared.
Together we celebrate the promises
that will be made today,
and ask that from them
joy and hope will flow.
Through Christ our Lord and Friend.
Amen

An all-age opening prayer for a wedding

Warm as the summer sunshine,
plentiful as the rain on the hills:
We praise you for your love, O Lord.

Gentle as the waves lapping the seashore,
powerful as the wind that bends the trees:
We praise you for your love, O Lord.

Deep as the gaze between two lovers,
forgiving as the friend who bears no grudge:
We praise you for your love, O Lord.

Caring as the parent holding their child,
comforting as the arms that embrace:
We praise you for your love, O Lord.

Strong as the bonds that draw us together,
never-ending as the circle that has no finish:
We praise you for your love, O Lord.
Amen

Keep us in your loving care (A responsive prayer)

O God, you created this world
to give it your love and companionship.
You long that all should know your care
and in you find shelter.
Gracious Lord,
keep us in your loving care.

O God, you are patient and slow to anger,
rich in kindness and faithful to your promises.
You never forget us, but in Jesus came into our world
to be alongside us in joy and sorrow.
Gracious Lord,
keep us in your loving care.

O God, we are the apple of your eye,
precious in your sight and loved eternally.
You shelter us under the shadow of your wings,
night and day, keep us all in your peace.
Gracious Lord,
keep us in your loving care.

O God, we pray for *(name)* and *(name)*
on this their wedding day:
bless their friendship, deepen their love
and fill this day with laughter.
Gracious Lord,
keep us in your loving care.
Amen

Prayers of intercession

A short prayer for the couple

We pray today for *(name)* and *(name)*,
asking your blessing upon them as they begin life together.

May they be a blessing to each other,
may they continue to bring happiness to one another
and always encourage the good in each other.
May they support, strengthen and comfort each other,
and in every situation in life
may they know, Lord,
that you guide and guard them.

Surround them with your presence always,
sustain their joy,
deepen their trust,
enfold them in your peace.
Amen

Prayer for the couple (inspired by 1 Corinthians 13)

Almighty God,
we pray that you will help *(name)* and *(name)*
to be true to the promises they have made
to one another today before you.
Inspire them with that vision of perfect love
that we know in Jesus Christ our Saviour.
Help them to show love that is patient,
kind and forgiving,
love that trusts, hopes and endures
through all things.

May they always remain open-hearted
and courageous;
give to them generosity of spirit,
understanding of each other
and the willingness to quickly forgive.

May they hold no grudges
but grow in warm and enduring friendship.

May their love be a sign of your love,
a blessing to each other and to those around them.
Through Christ our Guide and Hope.
Amen

For friendship

In their life together may *(name)* and *(name)* find many friends:
friends to show them kindness and concern,
friends to offer help and support,
friends who share smiles and laughter.

May they be a blessing to others,
a place where friendship can grow and blossom,
encouraging community to happen
and kindness to be shown.

Deepen *(name)* and *(name)*'s friendship,
that the love between them will stay strong.
And as they share that love with others,
may their concern help those who are lonely or sad.

For faith

Strengthen *(name)*'s and *(name)*'s trust in you,
that they may know you walk with them all their days.
Help them to look to you in all circumstances,
that in every aspect of their lives
they may be true to you and to each other.
May their shared faith and life
bring hope to others
as together they express the grace of God.

For children

We pray that you will bless *(name)* and *(name)* with the gift of children,
that you will grant them the privilege of bringing new life
from their life together.

Through the giving and receiving of care and affection in family life
bring them joy and fulfilment,
and the wisdom and perseverance to be good and kind parents.

For family

We pray for *(name)*'s and *(name)*'s families today,
in this moment both of letting go and taking in.
May they feel no sense of loss,
but instead the enrichment of their wider family life.

Out of their wisdom and experience
help them to know how they can support and encourage
(name) and *(name)* as they begin their life together.

For those in need

God, comfort those who today grieve for partner, family member or friend;
help them to cope with their loss,
encourage them with bright memories
and be near to them now and always.
We remember those who are lonely,
those who are wounded by relationship,
and those who long for a deeper companionship.

We pray for those who are unwell,
and those older friends not present
who find a day like this too much for them now.

Christ our peace,
today be with each one in their need.

Blessing for the close of a wedding service

May the way of Christ inspire us,
the love of Christ encourage us,
the light of Christ guide us,
and the peace of Christ go with us.

So may the blessing of God,
Creator, Saviour and Enabler,
be with us and those we hold in our hearts,
this day and always.
Amen

From dust to Easter dawn
Worship resources for Ash Wednesday

Rodney Aist

I. Responsive reading

Leader: Ash and rubble.
People: A lot of ash and rubble.

Leader: Sin, limitations and broken dreams …
People: … fill our lives, fill our streets, fill the world.

Leader: From ashes to ashes and dust to dust, life ends as it begins.
People: We can never escape the ash because the ash is us; the dust is ours.

Leader: Yet, ash, as dying life, becomes the soil of resurrection.
People: And in a world full of ashes, God imposes good news.

Leader: From the crossroads of human despair,
God invites us on a journey that transcends the dust.
People: From ashes to stars, from dust to Easter dawn.

Leader: Resurrection is rooted in what went wrong …
People: … and grows, through grace, into something gone right.

All: Amen

II. An Ash Wednesday reflection: A mount of ashes in Milan

Lent begins with ash and rubble and ends with a crucified body, sealed in a tomb, while pre-dawn darkness hovers over chaos and confusion. The pathway from Ash Wednesday to the threshold of resurrection is full of ash and rubble, which literally fill the streets in which we live.

I live on the corner of Monte Ceneri and Monte Generoso in Milan, Italy. The vast majority of Milanese streets are named after people, and I sense, as I walk, a city inhabited by the memory, legacy and shadows of the dead. Streets occasionally take the names of places instead of people – and here, in urban Milan, I live at an intersection named after two Swiss mountains.

We inhabit a world that is named after names, and I live, to be precise, on the corner of Mount Ashes (Ceneri) and Mount Generosity (Generoso), which, taken together, denotes heaps and heaps of cinders, embers and ruins

– a generosity of ashes, suggesting wasteland, destruction and desolation, atrocities and the worst images of human evil. I have yet to ascertain how Monte Ceneri, the mountain, got its name, and possibilities incite my imagination. Here, in the streets, at the intersection of place name and parable, there's no indication that people are aware of what the crossing means. Yet, their movements – much like our own – betray a search for meaning in a world layered with debris.

What I glimpse from my window – and enter whenever I go out – is human life in all its colour, in several shades of grey. Pedestrians, shoppers, loiterers and joggers. People coming and going, standing and waiting. Below multi-storied flats, there are bakeries, takeaways and phone shops. The post office queue extends down the street; there's always a crowd at the bus stop. Smells of pizza, dry cleaning and urine – not necessarily human – scent the air.

It's a paradox of place that the flattest of urban spaces can be named after mountains. Even so, Monte Ceneri takes urban horizons to a higher level: perched above the middle of the street for several hundred metres is an elevated viaduct shadowing life below. Up on the overpass, autos speed by, lorries roar and rumble and ambulances blare at regular intervals, spewing fumes and exhaust, spreading warnings and reminders. Life on Monte Ceneri is open, exposed and vulnerable; bifurcated, isolated and ignored. Ash settles on the ground.

While the corner of Monte Ceneri and Monte Generoso is completely flat, I'm a short walk away from Monte Stella (Mount Star), one of the higher points in the city. Atop its summit, one can see the Alps and glimpse the cathedral spires of Milan. Full of trees and verdant pathways, the park at Monte Stella is an urban interruption, a recreational paradise amidst the tarmac of Milan.

Monte Stella is no ordinary hill, beginning with the fact that it's named after the architect's wife, which betrays its life as an artificial mountain. Formed from the rubble of World War II, Monte Stella shines as a miracle of regeneration, a phoenix rising from its ashes, and its name – the Star Mountain – captures its celestial reach. With roots sunk into the soil of destruction, the trees of Monte Stella extend high into the sky, exuding life and beauty, offering shelter and protection, manifesting hope and resurrection.

If Ash Wednesday allows us to look ahead, it's a reminder that the cross is not discarded once the tomb is opened on Easter. Not as a fixation upon sin and death but precisely because its cinders are transformed into the soil of new life. Resurrection is rooted in rubble, and ash is a seed that, in its germination, conjoins heaven and earth.

While the bulk of my time is spent on Monte Ceneri, on the street of ashes, in the dust of everyday life, I'm grateful that Monte Stella is my neighbourhood park, amazed, as I walk, how God transforms the ruins of life. Reconciliation is rooted in what went wrong, and grows, through grace, into something gone right.

Of all Christian holy days, Ash Wednesday, which we mark with the imposition of ashes, is strangely the most familiar. To impose means 'to put or to place' but has further connotations of coming from an external source, as if what's being imposed is strange or foreign. While the imposition of ashes involves an external marking, the ashes themselves are too familiar to actually be imposed. The ashes we use include the combustion of our uniquely failed dreams, the embers of dashed hope, the exaltations of Palm Sundays gone wrong. The dust is composed of our ruined relationships, the debris of good intentions, the residue of our mistakes and failures. 'From ashes to ashes and dust to dust.' The words do not refer to some universal concept of inanimate matter nor is the dust from an outside source.

No, the ashes are us. The dust is the actualities of our lives. Our physical bodies. Our passions, limitations, mistakes and memories. Our families and friends. Our streets and neighbourhoods. The world in which we live. Our embodied journeys in time and place.

From ashes to ashes and dust to dust. The ash is specific, particular and familiar. It's messy, yet we know it – but what we may not know without the experience of an Easter sunrise on Monte Stella is that the dust of our lives is the soil of resurrection.

It's God who ultimately imposes, using the ash of our lives as the seed of new life. Lent is God's invitation to follow Jesus on a sacred journey from Monte Ceneri to Monte Stella, from everyday ashes to the starred summit of resurrection surprise. The mystery of Ash Wednesday is the strangely warm feeling that 'ashes to ashes' excites within us. Imbued with divine presence, the words are humbling, familiar, yet deeply comforting. As God's imposes good news upon us, we hear 'dust to dust' as a divine promise of God's pre-resurrection, providential care, and experience again for the first time the shadowed beginnings of the gospel story.

III. An Ash Wednesday prayer

God of chaos and cosmos, detritus and delight, we turn to you in a dirty and difficult moment, as life is confused and uncertain, fragile and disorienting. Life feels grounded (too grounded) but rootless, seeded but trampled, layered with soot. Instead of stretching towards the heavens, we feel buried, stuck and immobile. We began with lofty aspirations; now our eyes are on the ground. We are creatures of the soil on a sojourn of hibernation. Dust collects; waste accumulates, and residue remains. Ash inhabits our hearts.

The grit and grime of everyday life is exhausting, debilitating, and we seek cleansing, simplicity and purification. We long for newness, freshness, goodness and beauty. We long to begin again. Instead, you mark us with muck and tell us to wait. Our sanctuary is between a rock and a hard place. You whisper in our ear: 'Persevere.'

As you invite us on this Lenten journey, one of time as much as movement, the good news concerns method as much as meaning. You are not starting over with us, but using who we are, what we are, and where we are – dust, soot, ash and seed – on a journey of transformation. Things, to be sure, will remain sullied for a while. Instead of pristine vestments, the journey features sackcloth and will be stained with blood, sweat and tears. Yet, the miracle of Lent is the miracle of life: you take what is – as it is – and make it whole. You take us, as we are, and make us holy. The roots of resurrection are grounded in the ashes of today. And if Peter was with us, he'd declare on our behalf: 'Gracious God, do not mark only our heads with ash, but our hands and feet as well.' Ashes are prelude to the gospel journey, and that's good news!

In the name of the Father, Son and Holy Spirit. Amen.

The dust of life
An Ash Wednesday evening service

Thom M Shuman

Texts: Amos 5:8–15, Psalm 139:7–12, Romans 8:31–35, Luke 18:9–14

Call to worship:

We gather in the dimness of evening
to be with the God who brightens
the shadows of our lives.

We gather in the quiet of this place
to be with Jesus, knowing that nothing
past, present or future separates us.

We gather to be marked as disciples
to be fed for the journey through Lent,
to be sealed by the Spirit as God's own.

Evening prayer:

You wait on this evening,
Patient God,
for us to come back:
to stop going away from you
   on our self-focused travels;
to set aside our empty fears;
to cease shaping you in our image,
   so we can discover you closer
   than we ever dared imagine.

You wait for us this night,
Companion of our hearts,
for us to follow once more:
leaving the shuttered corners
   of our lives;
refusing to go from one failed
   promise to another;
coming out of the panic rooms
   we have built in our souls,
so you can take us by the hand
to lead us to resurrection life.

You wait in scattered ashes of our lives,
Spirit of silence,
for us to find you:
in the broken bread
   which strengthens us to serve;
in the cup of grace
   which fills our emptiness;
in our sisters and brothers
   who are willing to hold us up
   when we falter,
so you can embrace us
with joy and hope in every moment.

As you wait, and as we seek
to return to you in these moments,
we pray as we are taught:

(The Lord's Prayer)

Invitation to Lenten life:

Not for the first time, yet fresh once more,
we accompany Jesus to Jerusalem.

Because of his experience in the wilderness,
we discover how we might have the strength
to turn our back on evil, so we can choose good.

By his example of fasting and prayer,
in the midst of serving and caring for others,
we can learn that rhythm of faithful living
which allows us to work for justice and hope,
as we draw strength from the timeless acts
of silence, feasting on the word, and prayer.
As we remember our baptism into faith,
as we gather at the feast of grace,
as we are marked as Christ's own,
we prepare ourselves to come to God,
on this holy night.

Call to reconciliation:

On this night, we begin our journey to Easter. Before we can take the first step, we must admit how we have not been faithful to our God. Let us pray together, saying:

Unison prayer for forgiveness:

We have trouble telling the truth, God of broken hearts,
yet we must admit
on this night
how we have trouble being your people.

We may not trample the poor,
but we sometimes walk right past them.

We don't receive bribes,
but we are more privileged than many around us.

We trust more in ourselves than in you
and spend far too much time patting ourselves on the back,
rather than holding out a hand to others.

Where can we go for forgiveness but to you,
God of the ashes?

When we are greedy, you promise to be gracious.
When we have trouble confronting injustice, you stand at our side.

When we struggle to seek good,
you point us to Jesus, our Brother, our Saviour,
who shows us how to turn our back on evil
to follow him.
Amen

Silence is observed.

Assurance of pardon:

God refuses to stand far off, but comes close to us –
to hear our prayers, to touch our hearts with forgiveness
and to walk with us during this holy season and beyond.

**We have no need to go anyplace else
but into the comforting and restoring heart
of the One who loves us.
Thanks be to God.
We are forgiven.
Amen**

Imposition of the ashes:

Just yesterday it seems, the palms were
fresh and green, held tight in hands
as we re-enacted Jesus' entry into Jerusalem.

But then they dried, shrivelled, became
almost too fragile to touch, until
we burned them into the ashes for tonight.
Yet, by the grace of our God,
with the Spirit resting upon them,
they are mixed with oil and placed
on our heads or hands,
the dust of life resting upon us
as a sign that by sharing the gifts
of peace, reconciliation, justice and generosity,
we will live into the people we long to become.

As we are touched with this mark,
God of all moments,
remind us that just as you
shaped humanity from earth's dust,
so, from the ashes of repentance and denial,
that grace which is gifted to us

through Jesus Christ, our Redeemer,
will shape us into faithful followers.
Amen

(In the silence, those who wish may come to have the sign of the cross placed on their foreheads or back of their hands.)

Invitation to the Table

The Great Prayer of thanksgiving:

May the God of the ashes be with you.
And also with you.

On this night, let us offer our hearts to God.
We open them so we may be filled with the gifts of Lenten discipleship.

Let us lift glad thanksgiving to our God.
We offer praise to the One who gives us the strength for this journey.

There at the edge of the emptiness of chaos
you spoke, God of all graciousness,
   brightening the shadows with lights in the sky,
   pouring the waters into rivers and seas,
   planting seeds to feed all creatures.

From the dust of creation, you shaped your children,
offering us all the goodness and beauty
which overflowed from your heart;
   but we trampled through your hopes,
   as we turned from your heart
   to chase after evil's false promises.

But no matter where we went,
or how far we sought to flee from you,
you continued to meet us in all those places,
constantly inviting us to return to you
and be filled with your steadfast love.

Therefore, we join with our sisters and brothers,
in the silence and shadows of this evening,
to offer you songs of thanksgiving:

Holy, holy, holy are you, God who is at our side.
We join all creation in singing your praises.
Hosanna in the highest!

Blessed is the One who makes us right.
Hosanna in the highest!

Your constant love is the seal of your holiness,
and Jesus is the One who comes
so we will never be separated from you.
He endured every hardship we experience,
   so we receive the hope you offer to us;
he experienced the hunger of loneliness,
   so we might become members of your family;
he was willing to set aside his life,
   so death would have no power
   to keep us apart from you, but
   your resurrection power would give us
   the same life he received from you.

As we take our tentative first steps towards Jerusalem,
as we would be marked as his companions,
we remember that mystery known as faith:

Christ died, not withholding his heart.
Christ was raised, so that he might become our advocate.
Christ will come, to draw us to your side.

Here at this Table of life and longing,
pour out your Spirit on us,
and on the gifts offered to us.

May the bread which is broken
strengthen us so nothing can separate us
   from those who struggle with life;

from those who mourn a death;
from those who have no power or voice.

May the cup which overflows with grace
nourish us so we pick up
   those who have been trampled by misery;
   those who are trapped by injustice;
   those who are pushed aside by the privileged.

And when neither death nor life,
neither time nor history
can keep us apart from you
as you gather us around your Table
with our siblings of every time and place,
we will sing your glory and praise forever and ever,
God in Community, Holy and One. Amen

Sending:

Smudged this night with the ashes of penitence,
we will go out to share God's forgiveness
with those we have hurt, with those who are forgotten.

Fed this night by the Host of the Feast of grace,
we will go out to bring healing to the broken,
to offer grace to those trampled by the powerful.

Called this night to journey through suffering to new life,
we will go out to stand with those experiencing injustice,
to share the Spirit's peace and reconciliation with the world.

When I hear your voice
Stories, prayers and actions for International Women's Day

Janet Lees

Introduction

This resource is for a small group of women but can also be adapted for individual reflection, prayer and action. Although it is meant for a group of women, men can be part of the sharing too. However, please be aware that women need safe spaces. They need allies too, of course, but if the space has been designated for those identifying as female, then please respect that.

I am a storyteller, and when I tell stories I often begin with stories of women from my remembered Bible. Rather than read these stories out, try to tell them in your own way, or share the ones you remember. As you tell stories and share, you might like to make something together. Women around the world make things together in many ways – basketwork, sewing, knitting … But most of all, they make food. So you might like to invite folk to bring ingredients and make a meal together.

Feel free to adapt this resource as you need to and as fits your circumstances.

1. The three wise women

This could be told by three women.

When it came to lockdown the three wise women were no more ready than anyone else but they took their wisdom and shared what they could.

The first, a grandmother, shepherded her children and grandchildren through the pandemic. When the ups and downs came, she crested the waves with them, rejoicing at their birthday milestones celebrated from afar, and anxious when their exam results were subject to an ill-considered process or classrooms closed. But they made it through, at least as far as the next leap of trust and integrity.

The second, a widow, served the community with all her heart and mind and strength, shopping and supporting at all hours, on foot or on the phone. Fortunately she had a big heart and so in all that had gone on, although truly squeezed, it had not been crushed. Now was the time to share signs of hope and move on with new relationships.

The third, a priest, prayed as much as she could, keeping her day-night vigil. There were many Holy Innocents out there: anxious, vulnerable, alone. There were too many considered expendable by callousness and ignored by unkindness. Now, of all times, was the time for prayer.

Prayer:

Talk about women in your community and around the world who remind you of the three wise women. Give thanks for these women in a short prayer. For example:

Thank you, God,

for Carla, who is a kinship carer for her four grandchildren.

For Amara, who started the community telephone helpline.

For Esther at the church, who edits and sends out the newsletter …

Thank you for all wise women
in our communities
and in the community of your world.
Help us to support each other.
Amen

Action:

What symbols would you associate with the three wise women: the grandmother, the widow and the priest? As you speak of each wise woman, lay down those symbols, and then give participants a moment to think about them in silence, or to handle the symbols, if appropriate.

Or: In advance, invite participants to bring a symbol with them that speaks to them of grandmother, widow, priest. These could be shared during the retelling/reading of the stories.

On their travels the three wise women meet many other women. Some are bleeding, some are poor, some are homeless … These are some of those women's stories:

2. The bleeding woman

In a big crowd like this, I can be unnoticed. In a shapeless garment like this, I can be anonymous. But I bleed. I bleed all the time. I am the bleeding woman.

Constant bleeding makes a smell in this heat, or at least I think it does.

People shun me, move away, avoid me, or at least I think they do.

I think a touch would be enough. Just a slight fleeting touch such that no one would notice, except me. I'm not sure I can do it, get close enough, reach out.

I bleed. I bleed all the time. I am the bleeding woman.

It saps my energy, takes all of my strength and self-confidence with it. Each drop is another small loss, each small loss part of the bigger loss of who I am. There's not much left except that I am the bleeding woman.

Even other woman avoid me, don't look at me, stay back, or at least I think they do …

The touch, when I dare it, is tiny. A brush of a finger on the thread of the hem of a well-worn garment. But it is like a shock running up my arm – coursing through my limbs and turning off the flow.

We stop when he stops. The crowd pushing into each other, stumbling, cursing.

'Who touched me?' he asked.

How could he know? It was nothing. Barely a touch at all, not enough to register.

'Who touched me?' He knew. His eyes sought mine, but he was not accusing, only confirming.

'Go in peace,' he said.

I did. I may still bleed but the stigma is lifted. I am no longer beyond touching distance.

Prayer:

God of many transformations,
lover, parent, friend:
as we go on, one worn body to another,
may we cherish each cell and microbe,
value each creature, bright and beautiful,
touch the earth gently and reverently,
love each neighbour, sentient and unthinking,
in the ongoing dance,
in the name of the Holy One-in-Three.

Action:

'Bloody Good Period' works to end period stigma and period poverty. You can read about their work and get involved through:

www.bloodygoodperiod.com

3. The widow

She shuffled into the temple, back and head bent over, looking down. At one time she'd have looked up, stunned and amazed, but she was done with awe. She was here for the living, not the dead: she'd done with memory. It was too corrosive, too painful. These days she found silence everywhere, tripped over it in the streets and alleyways, came across it piled up in corners of the house, saw it in her neighbours' faces, and here in the temple. What was there to say? Who was there to say it? Silence reigned, and there are many kinds of silence.

Over there she saw him, sitting watching. His face too was silent, but not blank like her neighbours' faces. His face held the silence comfortably and his body wore it naturally, as if silence was a long-held habit from which he had grown and was flowering this very day.

His silence warmed her for a bit. There was in it a small spark that said to her that hope was still possible. She looked down into the palm of her hand and the coins seemed to glow, which was odd as they had been very dull when she put them there earlier in the morning.

All she had to live on – things were getting desperate. What would happen next? Where would the next meal come from?

Shuffling to the offertory box, she let the two small coins drip from her palm into the darkness. She heard two very small clinks of metal hitting something else in the bottom of the box. Can't go back now: can't get them out. She shrugged; maybe her family and neighbours would think her mad, but it was her decision. She lifted up her head and straightened her back, creaking inside herself as she unwrapped her habitual posture.

It would have to do. She walked back out into the silent sunlight bathing the silent streets, and watched the silent faces at the silent windows.

Another hour, another day: all she had to do was live on.

Prayer:

God of hour and day,
catch us up in your timeless love,
that the desperate may find hope
in the small acts of kindness we offer.
In the silence we recall every woman,
the named and unnamed:
may each spark burn brighter.

Action:

You may want to make your own offering here: perhaps a donation to a group combatting poverty, for example the Women's Budget Group, which 'puts forward policies for a more gender-equal future and builds the capacity of women and women's groups to participate in economic debates':

https://wbg.org.uk

Or perhaps you'd like to make a pledge to volunteer with a women's group or refuge in your local area.

4. Prayer of a well-housed woman

This piece originally appeared in French in a magazine about homelessness which featured stories of homeless women.

The well-housed woman lived in a house of brick,
with strong foundations and efficient heating.
The well-housed woman looked out of her double-glazed windows
on a world of chaos and chance.
The well-housed woman sorted her way through
her boxes of surplus items, and tried to pray.

The unhoused woman laid out her sleeping bag in the damp doorway,
stuffing her belongings into the split carrier bags.
The unhoused woman heard the street sounds around her
and felt the broken pavement under her.
The unhoused woman felt vulnerable and afraid
as another night advanced, and tried to pray.

The well-housed woman had seen the sleeping bag in the doorway,
the split carrier bags and damp newspaper.
The well-housed woman had turned up her collar
against the incoming gale and stinging rain.
The well-housed woman had held on to her shopping,
her phone and her purse, and tried to pray.

The unhoused woman turned over, coughing,
and saw the shoes of the well-housed woman.
The unhoused woman wanted the well-housed woman
to leave her alone and so she turned her back.
The unhoused woman didn't want pity but a way through
to something like security, and tried to pray.

I am the well-housed woman.
I live in a house;
you sleep in a doorway:
How can I pray tonight?

Prayer:

Companion Christ, who walked the streets,
but also knew the welcome of a warm home:
the changes we need to make,
so that everyone has a home,
mean tearing down our old haunts
and building new places
where doors stand open and all are kin.
Help us to believe that we can live
the life to which you call us,
and build thriving communities
where all are welcome.

May the angels keep watch tonight.

Action:

Give each participant a brick-shaped piece of paper, and ask folk to write or draw on it the things they think are needed to help build a fairer 'kindom'.[1] For example: 'Equal pay', 'mental health resources', 'affordable child care', 'support for refugees and asylum seekers' …

Afterwards, assemble the bricks together into the shape of a dwelling.

Then repeat the last lines of the prayer together:

Help us to believe that we can live
the life to which you call us,
and build thriving communities
where all are welcome.

You might want to send a donation to a homelessness charity, or read about their work.

5. When I hear your voice, I rejoice

We are listening for the voices of women.

Some are far away, some are nearby.

Share the names of women in your community and around the world who are working to make a difference. Then respond together with the words: 'When I hear your voice, I rejoice.'

For example:

Greta Thunberg,
when I hear your voice, I rejoice.

Jacinda Ardern,
when I hear your voice, I rejoice.

Vera, who serves so calmly and helpfully at the Co-op checkout,
when I hear your voice, I rejoice.

Padma, who runs the Community Garden,
when I hear your voice, I rejoice …

For possible reference:

BBC list of 100 inspiring and influential women from around the world

And/or search on the Internet for inspirational women throughout history.

6. Blessing of the God of Rahab

There are many ways to bless.

Rahab the prostitute is mentioned as having lived in Jericho, and people probably kept their distance from her. Sex work is like that: a lot of people avoid you. Jesus knew this and made it clear that prostitutes were welcome in God's 'kindom'. He asked questions about sexual behaviour, but not in the way which was expected at the time. Rather than condemning a woman accused of adultery, he told her accusers to examine their own behaviour first.

Later, at the beginning of Matthew's Gospel, Rahab was remembered amongst the women who were ancestors of Jesus.

Rahab was instructed to use a red thread as a way of sending a message out of the besieged city of Jericho. Amongst the different symbolic meanings associated with a red thread is solidarity amongst women, especially those silenced or socially avoided.

Take a red ribbon, cloth or string and tie it to a window latch or door handle.

Think of women who are silenced or shunned. Talk about this.

Then read this blessing together:

May the God of Rahab the prostitute bless you.
May Christ, conceived by Mary, bless you.
May the Holy Spirit, recogniser of the red thread, bless and affirm you.
And may you, and all your sisters, be a blessing to each other.

7. Further time of sharing and being together

You may want to add music, songs or art to your time together. Focus on the voices of women. Or share your own poems, songs, art, recipes, craftwork, DIY, photographs, hobbies, campaigning work, gardening … Share something that you're proud of; that expresses something of who you are … Pour another cup of tea and enjoy your time together.

Possible resource:

www.internationalwomensday.com

Note:

1. The word 'kindom' is used to indicate a gender-equal community.

We shout out their names and honour their courage

A reflection and prayer for the UN International Day of Remembrance of the Victims of Slavery and the Transatlantic Slave Trade (25th March)

Iain and Isabel Whyte

Reflection

On the 27th of March 2007, two thousand of us were in Westminster Abbey at a service marking the 200th anniversary of the Abolition of the Slave Trade by Britain. The Queen and the Duke of Edinburgh were there, as were Prime Minister Tony Blair, Chancellor Gordon Brown and representatives of many organisations. Toyin Agbetu, founder of Ligali, a Pan African group that challenges racism and imperialism, got up from his seat and walked to the crossing. He addressed the dignitaries in a speech that was certainly not part of the intended programme. Before being led out he reminded us that the three major institutions involved in slavery were the monarchy, the government and the Church, and called on all African Christians present to walk out as a protest against this 'insult'.

Next year at the Edinburgh Festival of Spirituality I had the chance to meet this friendly, courteous and passionate man and to discuss with him the gaps in the history of resistance to slavery – those who liberated themselves and helped their sisters and brothers to do likewise.

It is as temptingly easy to see those who suffered for hundreds of years under what many Africans see as their 'Holocaust' – and which certainly ranks as one of the greatest crimes against humanity – as victims, with the passivity that this implies. It is equally tempting (and this was partly what angered Toyin Agbetu so much) to give exclusive credit for the ending of slavery to principled white men, many of them Christian. Most people know about William Wilberforce or Abraham Lincoln, Thomas Clarkson or David Livingstone, all of whom made significant contributions. But only recently have we started to honour folk like Harriet Tubman in the United States, Sam Sharpe in Jamaica, James McCune Smith in Scotland or Tula Rigaud in the Dutch West Indies.

Harriet Tubman liberated herself from slavery in Maryland in 1849 and made no less than thirty-six journeys back south at huge risk of re-enslavement to help others become liberated and reach the safety of Canada through the famous 'Underground Railroad', the network of guides and safe houses staffed by black and white abolitionists. She was nicknamed 'Moses' and her contemporary Frederick Douglass said to her that he knew of no one who willingly encountered more perils and hardships to liberate enslaved people than her. In 2021 the Biden administration revived a proposal to have her portrait on the new US $20 notes.

Sam Sharpe was a Baptist preacher in Jamaica, the largest slave island in the British Caribbean. Scottish and English missionaries were forbidden by their societies to get involved in 'political issues' such as emancipation, and Britain was still delaying the parliamentary action. In 1831 Sharpe led a strike of all enslaved people on the island, which led to a full-scale rebellion. He and hundreds of others were executed but the severe reprisals led to public outcry in Britain and there is little doubt that the Sharpe uprising hastened the legal end of plantation slavery two years later.

James McCune Smith was born into slavery in 1813. Unable to study medicine in the USA, he travelled to Scotland and graduated MD from Glasgow University as top student in his year in 1837. Whilst a student he was a valued committee member of the Glasgow Emancipation Society campaigning for the abolition of the notorious Apprenticeship Scheme which was slavery by another name in the West Indies. On his return to America he became a leading intellectual in the anti-slavery movement until his death a month before slavery was abolished there. A café off the city's High Street is named after him, and in 2019 the James McCune Smith Learning Hub in Glasgow University was opened.

In 1795 Tula Rigaud, an enslaved plantation worker, challenged the colonial governor with the bold assertion that all humans were the descendants of Adam and Eve. He assured him that those who rose up at that time did not want to harm anyone but simply sought their freedom. Tula was inspired by the French Revolution, and he took his last name from a hero of the successful Haitian Revolution in 1791. A month after the uprising Tula was forced into hiding but was betrayed and sentenced to death. Today there are statues to Tula in Curaçao, where he is a national hero and the uprising is celebrated every August, and in Winschoten near Groningen in the northern Netherlands.

These are just snapshots of the hidden history of resistance to the tyranny of slavery. We need also to remember the unsung millions who risked torture, if not death, to free themselves and their families, and who gave much through their humanity and their faith all these years ago to ensure that 'Black Lives Matter'. Many used spirituals such as 'Steal away to Jesus' and 'Break bread together' as codes to inspire and instruct others on the journey to freedom.

Iain Whyte

Prayer

In the presence of the God of freedom,
we remember:

the people who have stood firm,
those who have not turned away,
those who have taken risks,
who have laid their own lives on the line.

The campaigners, the changemakers,
the lovers of truth, of peace, of justice.
Those who have faced their fears,
who have broken the silence and stood firm
in the face of tyranny, persecution and the lust for power.
Those who have shamed racism and the many 'isms'
which are used to 'excuse' human prejudice.

We shout out their names and honour their courage:
Harriet Tubman, Rosa Parks, Sojourner Truth,
Frederick Douglass, Tula Rigaud, Sam Sharpe,
James McCune Smith, Martin Luther King …
And all those who liberated themselves and helped
others on the road to freedom.
We pause and give thanks for all those whose names we don't know
but whose struggles and triumphs we honour.

In the presence of the God of Freedom, Truth and Justice,
we affirm that Black Lives Matter and that we will all
break bread together.

Isabel Whyte

The silent stars howl in grief
A liturgy for Passion Sunday

Thom M Shuman

Texts: Isaiah 50:4–9a; Psalm 31:9–16; Philippians 2:5–11; Matthew 26:14–27:66

Litany of the Passion:

What shall we do with you, Jesus?
**Glad songs sung at your birth
will turn to jeers, taunts, and worse,
hurled at you from every side.**

What shall we do with you, Jesus?
**We will promise to stay,
but then run away;
we will sleep through
the anguish of your heart.**

What shall we do with you, Jesus?
**The One who gave living waters
to an outsider at a well,
the One baptised in the Jordan
will thirst upon a tree.**

What shall we do with you, Jesus?
**Before this week runs its course,
the disciples, including even us,
will fail you in force.**

Silence is kept.

Lamb of God, you cry out in agony:
and the silent stars howl in grief.

Lamb of God, you breathe your last:
and the Spirit moves over the void in our hearts.

Lamb of God, you are placed in a cold tomb:
**and creation trembles in the deep,
even as we pray as we are taught:**

(The Lord's Prayer)

Call to reconciliation:

What shall we do with our sins?
Shall we continue to try to hide them, or confess them –
honestly and without reservation –
to the One who comes to vindicate us?
Join me as we pray together, saying:

Unison prayer for forgiveness:

**We confess, Passionate God,
how often we scheme against you.
In every moment,
we look for chances to betray you,
breaking your heart.**

**We turn our backs on those
who reach out to us for help.**

**We hide our faces from those
who are wasting away from hopelessness.**

**Be gracious to us, Compassionate God,
and stay with us in these moments.
Morning by morning,
awaken us with your voice of mercy,
and call us to humble ourselves in service to others,
as did Jesus Christ, our Lord and Saviour.
Amen**

Silence is kept.

Assurance of pardon:

It is God who holds our lives,
healing us when we are broken,
forgiving us when we do wrong.
Our tongues have confessed,

**now let our hearts and lives reflect the One
who humbled himself for us.
Amen**

Prayer of dedication/offering:

Your passion for justice for the most vulnerable,
of hope for the despairing
and of life for every single one of us
is the model we seek to live.
In your name, we pray, Lamb of God.
Amen

Great prayer of thanksgiving:

May the God of Holy Week be with you.
And also with you.

Join your hearts with the One whose
heart breaks in pieces this week.
We offer them for healing and hope.

With songs too painful to sing,
with sighs too deep to utter.
We lift our mournful souls to God.

When the hour was at hand,
you called forth creation, Holy God,
your Word teaching
    the birds what to sing,
    the butterflies where to flit,
    the grass how to grow,
    the trees how to stand straight and tall.

You did all this for us,
your children created in your image,
asking us to stay with you forever.
But we asked of sin and death

what they would give us to betray you,
    and went running off, our pockets
    filled with their 30 pieces of seduction.

Deeply grieved, you continued to call
through the prophets of every generation,
but they always found us sleeping,
    wearied by our foolish choices.

You sent Jesus to us, to awaken us
to his voice of gentleness and grace.
With those who have spent their lives in sorrow,
with those who bow their knees to you,
we offer our prayers to you:

Holy, holy, holy are you, God who is gracious to us.
All creation trusts in your promises.
Hosanna in the highest!

Blessed is the One who will not desert us.
Hosanna in the highest!

Your heart was broken, Vindicator of our lives,
by the pain and suffering of your Son, Jesus.
Of one mind with you, he came
    so we might rethink our foolish choices.
Leaving glory behind in the closet,
    he became human like us,
    so we might see you face to face.
Without the promise of any reward,
though he felt abandoned by you,
    he willingly went to the cross,
    his life poured out for those who
    mocked him, spat on him, betrayed him.

Yet, when sin thought Jesus
was safely sealed into the tomb,
swaddled in death's tight bands,
    you did not let him be put to shame,

but called him forth into the morning,
with Resurrection's kiss.

As we journey with him through this holiest of weeks,
as we betray him and abandon him,
we are sustained by that mystery called faith:

Christ died, the world having washed its hands of him.
Christ was raised, your hands breaking death's strong grip on him.
Christ will come, to take us by the hand and lead us to you.

Here in this place, we gather
for that meal which signifies
brokenness as well as healing,
heartbreak as well as hope.

What should we do with the Bread?
We will let its life strengthen us
to go forth to serve those
  whom the world has betrayed
  with broken promises and hollow words.

What shall we do with the Cup?
We will drink deeply of it
so we can empty ourselves
  for those whose lives are
  spent from grief and fear.

And when we drink of the
fruit of the vine with our
siblings from every time and place,
we will bow our knees in worship,
extolling you forever and ever,
God in Community, Holy and One.
Amen

Sending:

As you leave this place, go as God's children:
We will go to serve our siblings.

Go as followers of Christ:
**We will find the broken around us
and bring them healing.**

Go as those strong in the Spirit:
**We will humble ourselves
for those wearied by life.**

Like cloaks laid on the ground
A liturgy for Palm Sunday

Thom M Shuman

Texts: Isaiah 50:4–9a; Psalm 118:1–2, 19–29; Philippians 2:5–11; Matthew 21:1–11

Call to worship (Matthew 21:1–11, NRSV):

Voice one: When they had come near Jerusalem
and had reached Bethphage, at the Mount of Olives,
Jesus sent two disciples, saying to them,

Voice two: 'Go into the village ahead of you,
and immediately you will find a donkey tied,
and a colt with her;
untie them and bring them to me.
If anyone says anything to you, just say this,
"The Lord needs them."
And he will send them immediately.'

Voice one: This took place to fulfil
what had been spoken through the prophet, saying,

All: Tell the daughter of Zion,
'Look, your king is coming to you, humble,
and mounted on a donkey,
and on a colt, the foal of a donkey.'

Voice two: The disciples went and did as Jesus had directed them;
they brought the donkey and the colt,
and put their cloaks on them, and he sat on them.

A very large crowd spread their cloaks on the road,
and others cut branches from the trees
and spread them on the road.
The crowds that went ahead of him and that followed
were shouting,

All: 'Hosanna to the Son of David!
Blessed is the one who comes in the name of the Lord!
Hosanna in the highest heaven!'

Voice one: When he entered Jerusalem,
the whole city was in turmoil, asking,
'Who is this?'

The crowds were saying,

All: 'This is the prophet Jesus from Nazareth in Galilee.'

Prayer of the day:

God of hopes and joys,
when our hearts ache from brokenness,
you nourish us with your love;
when the world's pain fatigues us,
you carry us in your arms;
when the loneliness of our souls
drains our very being,
you come and live with us.
You are our God.

Jesus Christ,
God's True Son,
you did not profit
from your Oneness with God,
but emptied yourself
to become servant to all humanity.
You humbled yourself
to lift us out of sin's grave.
You are our Lord.

Holy Spirit,
Teacher from God,
humble us to be obedient and to
deny and reject
all that keeps us from following Jesus;
teach us the words we need
to confess him as our Lord and Saviour.
You are our Helper.

God in Community, Holy and One,
we lift our prayer to you as Jesus has taught us,
saying:

(The Lord's Prayer)

Call to reconciliation:

One day we are crying to God, 'Save us',
the next we are turning our backs on God
and walking away.
Despite our fickle nature,
God is steadfast in loving us and constant in forgiving us.
Let us confess to our God, as we pray:

Unison prayer for forgiveness:

**With joy in our hearts,
we welcome your servant, O God,
only to reject him when he picks up a cross
instead of a crown.**

**Like cloaks laid on the ground before Jesus,
we pick up our faith,
dust it off
and put it back in the closet until we need it.
We can be as stubborn and rebellious
as the city which cheers your name.**

**Save us, Redeeming God, save us!
May we lay our doubts,
our fears,
our worries,
our weariness
at your feet,
trusting and believing
that you will forgive what is sinful,
make whole our brokenness**

and welcome us as sisters and brothers
of our Lord and Saviour, Jesus Christ.
Amen

Assurance of pardon:

Hosanna to David's Son!
Blessed is the One who comes in God's name,
not to judge us, but to save us.
**We humble ourselves in gratitude to God
and in service to others, as Christ did.
Hosanna in the highest!
Amen!**

Prayer of dedication/offering:

We could triumphantly claim that you came just for us,
Holy One,
but your gifts are poured out for all the broken,
all the wandering,
all the struggling.
So, may we be just like you,
pouring out our lives and our treasures,
so all might be blessed through you, we pray.
Amen

Great prayer of thanksgiving:

The Lord of parades be with you.
And also with you.

People of God, open your hearts
to the One who comes with hope.
**We receive the joy and grace
the prophet from Nazareth brings us.**

Give thanks to God, for God's love endures forever!
God is our God, the One who comes to make us whole.

Joy is indeed the highest praise
we can offer to you,
Steadfast Love.

On that first morning,
you woke creation
    from its slumbering sleep,
      to give light to chaos' shadows.
Morning by morning,
you shaped your dreams
    into everything that is true,
      turning hopes into your justice.
You asked simply that we rejoice
in your gifts and glory;
    but we chose to sing the choruses
    of sin and rebellion,
      following death as it paraded
      through the world.

Prophets struggled to awaken
our dulled ears
with whispers of peace,
    but we laughed at their ideas
    that we should return to you.
When you could have set your face like flint,
when you could have hardened your resolve,
you sent your Child, your Joy.

Therefore, we join our voices in thanksgiving
with those who shouted 'Hosanna'
and with those who ran away from you,
with those in every moment,
and in this moment,
singing with all creation to your glory:

Holy, holy, holy are you, Opener of our ears.
All creation proclaims,
'God's steadfast love endures forever.'
Hosanna in the highest!

**Blessed is the One who opens the gates of righteousness.
Hosanna in the highest!**

You are holy, God our Creator,
and blessed is Jesus Christ,
who comes in your grace.

When he could have filled your heart,
    he poured himself out for us;
when he could have remained by your side,
    he came to be a servant, raising us to glory;
when he could have watched from heaven,
    he came down to show us your heart;
when he could have taken the easy way,
    he chose to be faithful to you,
        even to the point of shameful death.
As he gathered up our brokenness
to make us whole,
you raised him to new life,
    and he stands with us in eternity,
        glorifying you forever.

As we remember the joy and excitement of the parade,
as we remember the gentle words he taught,
as we remember the spirit with which he died,
we proclaim the One who is the Bread of Life:

**Christ died, emptying his life for us.
Christ was raised, defeating our old adversaries sin and death.
Christ will come, to fulfil what has been promised.**

Here, at this Table,
we receive the gifts
of the bread and the cup,
and your Spirit which anoints us with peace.

Nourish us with the Bread of hope,
    that we might go into
        the brokenness of our world;

fill us with the cup of grace,
    so the weary will discover us
    standing by their side;

fill us with the overflowing joy
of the good news,
    so we might sing forever
    of your heart's desire
    for justice and peace for all people.

Then, on that final morning,
when we gather for the Feast of the Lamb,
when we are seated with those
who shouted their hosannas,
as well as those who yelled for death,
we will join our voices in eternity's anthem,
giving our thanks to you forever and ever,
God in Community, Holy and One.
Amen

Sending:

The One wounded by the nails in our hearts sends us forth,
to bring healing with God's love.

The One who continues on the journey invites us to follow,
cradling the broken hearts of the world as we go.

The One whose Spirit is in the Kingdom-Bearer fills us with hope,
if we but trust in the promises of this day.

Note:

Passages from NRSV copyright 1989, Division of Christian Education of the National Council of the Churches of Christ in the United States of America. Used by permission. All rights reserved.

Remembering mothers
Resources for Mother's Day

Tom Gordon

For mothers everywhere

I'm mothered by my mother … of course, you know that's true.
No need to think I'm different! I'm just the same as you.
It's what we have in common. So, I'm on solid ground.
I'm mothered by my mother, now Mother's Day's come round.

I'm mothered by my father! 'You're what?' I hear you say.
But constancy and nurture have always been his way.
So, when I think of mothers, I pray for fathers too.
I'm mothered by my father … so, is that the same for you?

I'm mothered in my friendships: those folk who're always there,
who take the time to listen, who show me that they care,
with comfort when I need it, and laughter as they should.
I'm mothered in my friendships with mothering that's good.

I'm mothered in community, the places where I'm bound
in common cause and purpose with people who're around
to share concerns and pleasures, and carry me along.
I'm mothered in community, for that's where I belong.

I'm mothered by a presence – 'God' is the name I choose,
though other names and concepts may be the ones you use.
I know that there is something around me every day.
I'm mothered by a presence … that's all that I can say.

A mother and a father, and special, faithful friends,
communities of nurture, a Love that never ends …
So pause, just for a moment, and join me in a prayer,
now Mother's Day is with us, for mothers everywhere.

Giving thanks for mothers

Jochebed was a mother, a Levite, who gave birth to a child.
A fine son, she called him, but feared for his well-being.
So she hid him, and watched him, and gave him to a new life.
Jochebed was the mother of Moses, a flawed man but a great leader.
A mother who gave life to the prospect of freedom, hope and promise.

Amathlai was a mother, married to Terah, who gave birth to a child.
A brave women she was, so legend tells us and the sages assure us,
ready to defy her husband and her king to save the babe she was carrying.
Amathlai was the mother of Abraham, God's man, patriarch of his people.
A mother who gave life to obedience, service, belief and faith.

An unnamed woman, lost in the mists of time, gave birth to a child,
an orphaned daughter, given to a cousin, Mordecai, for nurture and growth.
A queen, she became, challenging prejudice, stereotypes, gender bias.
An unnamed woman was the mother of Esther, who faced fear with strength.
A mother who gave life to newness, though she never saw the result.

Bathsheba, wife of King David, gave birth to a child,
the sins of a mother and the failures of a father put to one side,
when force of circumstance and opportunity saw a son's personality triumph.
Bathsheba was the mother of Solomon, one of the greats in a long line.
A mother who gave life to wisdom, which made its mark for all time.

Mary, betrothed to Joseph, gave birth to a child,
not hers alone, but a Son given to the whole world for time and eternity.
'You shall call his name Emmanuel,' she was told, 'for this is God with us.'
Mary was the mother of Jesus, Holy Mary, mother of God himself.
A mother who gave life to Love, and Joy, and Peace, and Blessedness.

Remembering mother again

Remembering mother is always a joy,
going all the way back to when I was a boy,
and now, as an adult, with thoughts to enjoy …
I'm remembering mother again.

Remembering mother brings tears when I pause
and think of occasions when I was the cause
of heartbreak – and she remained just as she was …
I'm remembering mother again.

Remembering mother when scoldings she gave
to someone who never knew how to behave
the way that she wanted – but still she forgave …
I'm remembering mother again.

Remembering mother who dried all my tears,
and soothed me, and calmed me, removing my fears,
who never gave up on me all through the years …
I'm remembering mother again.

Remembering mother with pleasure and pride,
in things that I speak of, and more that's implied.
Wherever she is now, she's still by my side …
I'm remembering mother again.

Remembering mother, and joining with you
to offer the thanks and the praise that is due
to everyone's mother, on Mother's Day too,
and remembering mothers again.

Remembering mum

I remember my mum …
one night, when I couldn't sleep (I must have been six or seven)
and I came downstairs for a glass of milk, and the living room light was on,
when everyone was supposed to be in bed.
You had to go through the living room to get to the kitchen in our house.
And I found my mother sitting in my dad's chair by the fire,
reading her big, red, floppy Bible.
'Can't sleep, eh?' she said. 'Neither can I. Neither can I.
So God and I decided to have some time together.
Want to join in for a bit?'
So I did as she wanted, me and my mum and her God,
in my dad's chair in our living room –
after I had my milk, of course.

I remember my mum …
one evening, when I couldn't be bothered (I'd be about nineteen)
but I had to go to the church hall to collect her, after a social event,
when everything was supposed to be finished.
My mum was at the church for all kinds of reasons –
and not just on Sundays – doing things for other people.
But she wasn't ready, not for ages.
'Still lots to do … running late … sit down for a while.'
So, I sat and waited, and tolerated the delay,
as she buzzed around with trays of cakes, serving, helping.
I waited, just as she wanted (no idea where God was)
till she was ready to come home –
after I'd had two fairy-cakes, of course.

I remember my mum …
when my second daughter was born (I wasn't yet twenty-nine)
and I came home from work, when my folks were on holiday with us,
and the baby hadn't been sleeping.
I can see it now as clear as day – my mum, who wasn't too well,
and my little girl who wasn't crying any more,
together, bonded, as one.
'You're so like my mum,' I'm proud to tell that adult child now.

My mum and my children are bound together.
Genetics, perhaps, who knows, or maybe just all mixed up in my head.
I'm not bothered really, and God isn't either.
It's enough she's still in them, and I thank God for that –
after I've smiled a lot, of course.

I remember my mum …
in a hospital bed, the night before her operation (I'd just turned thirty),
flushed she was, but not frightened.
'In the hands of the surgeon and in the hands of my Maker,' she said,
never losing her faith for one moment.
She said it all, while I was tongue-tied.
And I never saw her again, alive, and well, and busy, and loving.
'I miss you and I love you …' Every day I tell her.
She and God decided to have some more time together.
And, from time to time, I join in.
I do what she always wanted, me and my mum and our God together,
in an eternal bond of loving memory –
after I've cried again, of course.

What is a mother?

A mother
holds you in her very being
until it's time to share you with a waiting world.

A mother
suckles you with the milk of love,
and would give you all that she has of her life.

A mother
teaches you, from the very start, by her smile
that love makes the world a good place to be.

A mother
cleans you, and protects you, sorts you and clothes you,
giving up her own time to make it your time.

A mother
watches you grow, picks you up when you fall,
and encourages you to try, again and again and again.

A mother
holds your hand, firmly but gently at the same time
and guides you in her way, but both of you as one.

A mother
scolds you and forgives you in one breath,
in one embrace of her heart, and soul, and mind, and strength.

A mother
lets you go when she would rather go with you,
worries about you, till you are safe, and well, and home again.

A mother
waits for you, yearns for you, hopes for you,
even when you don't remember that you mean so much to her.

A mother
is always your home, in safety and welcome,
not confined to place, or time, or circumstance.

A mother
weeps for you, in sorrow and in pride,
sometimes in secret, sometimes with you in her arms.

A mother
shares you with everyone else, gives you away to life and love,
yet you are always hers, completely, without condition.

A mother
knows you, often better than you know yourself,
and in words and silence shows she believes in you.

A mother
loves you, uniquely, exceptionally, more than she loves herself,
in understanding and mystery, in time and eternity.

A mother
has done what she wanted to do in her very being –
gave you life, so you can change the world for good.

Go out into the darkness
A tenebrae for Maundy Thursday evening

Janet Lees

This reflective service has been used in all-age worship with children aged 9-14 years.[1]

During this service candles are extinguished to symbolise the way Jesus was abandoned by everyone on the night before his death.

Tenebrae is a Latin word that means 'darkness'.

For this service you will need:

Seven unlit candles (placed on a large central table), a means of lighting them and a candle snuffer; a bunch of coins; a plate of bread and a cup of wine or juice (placed on the central table); a hammer, nails and a piece of wood to bang them into.

Readers and actors: Readers 1 and 2, Disciple 1, Jesus, Judas, Peter, other disciples (James, John …). These parts may be played by people of any gender.

Opening words (from Psalm 139):

Reader 1: If I say, 'Surely the darkness shall cover me, and everything around me becomes like night', even the darkness is not dark to you; the night is bright as the day, for dark and light are the same with you.

Opening responses:

Reader 2: In a week when passions run high –
confusion, anger, fear, doubt …
**Help us, travelling Christ,
to go with you on the road
into the unknown night.**

Reader 2: Give to us the Spirit of adventure so that
where there is confusion,
Patterns may emerge.

Reader 2: Where there is anger,
Love may spring up anew.

Reader 2: Where there is fear,
Calm may prevail.

Reader 2: Where there is doubt,
**We may find faith again.
Amen**

Song or chant

Reading/drama:

> *Use this, or create your own retelling, in whatever style (work on this in a group).*
>
> *You could act this out or read it: adapt to your location, community. Be creative.*

Reader 2: On the night of his arrest, Jesus kept the Passover meal with his friends. We will follow the journey that Jesus made and remember what happened to him on that night.

On the first day of the Passover Festival, the disciples came to Jesus.

Disciple 1: We're going to get everything ready for the Passover meal. Where do you want us to hold it?

Jesus: Go into Jerusalem. To a man I know there. Tell him the teacher says, 'The time is near. I will have the meal in your home with my friends.'

The seven candles are lit by Disciple 1, to represent the candles lit for the Passover meal.

Reader 1: In the evening, Jesus was sitting at the table with the twelve. Everyone was eating, drinking and talking.

Jesus: Well, you may be surprised to hear this, but tonight one of you will hand me over to my enemies.

Reader 2: They were all very shocked and sad to hear this.

Disciples: Lord – surely it's not me!

Jesus: The one who has dipped his bread into the same bowl as me will be the one to do it.

Judas: Teacher, surely it's not *me* you're referring to?

Jesus: Yes. It is you.

Judas drops some coins onto the table, extinguishes the 1st candle and leaves the room.

Reader 1: While they continued eating, Jesus took some bread, and said a prayer of thanks to God for it. Then he tore off some pieces, handed them to his friends, and said:

Jesus: Take this bread and eat. It is my body.

Reader 2: Then he took a cup of wine, and said thanks, and passed it to them, saying:

Jesus: Drink a sip of this wine. It is my blood. My blood which will be poured out to forgive the sins of the world and begin the new understanding between God and his people. I will not drink this wine again until the day when we are all gathered together in my Father's kingdom.

Reader 1: Then they all sang a song, and then went out together to the Mount of Olives.

Song or chant

Disciple 1 extinguishes the 2nd candle.

Jesus: Tonight you will all be so afraid, you will lose your faith in me. The scriptures say, 'I will kill the shepherd, and the sheep will scatter.' I will be crucified, but after three days I will rise from death. Then I will go to Galilee. I'll be travelling ahead of you and will meet you there.

Peter: Jesus, all of the other followers here may lose their faith in you – but *my* faith in you will remain as strong as ever! Solid as a rock.

Jesus: The truth is, Peter, tonight you will say that you don't even know me. You will deny me three times before the cock crows.

Peter: Jesus, I would *never* say I don't know you! I would die for you!

Peter extinguishes the 3rd candle.

Reader 2: Then Jesus went with his friends to the Garden of Gethsemane.

Jesus: Sit here and rest while I go and pray.

Reader 1: He took Peter, James and John with him. He was very upset.

Jesus: I am so sad, I feel as if my heart is breaking, as if my life is ending. Please, sit beside me and stay awake with me.

Reader 2: After a while Jesus went off by himself. He fell to his knees and prayed:

Jesus: Father, if it is possible, take this cup away from me. But not my will, your will.

Reader 1: Then he went back to his friends, and found them all sleeping.

Jesus: Couldn't you stay awake with me? To pray for strength. You want to do the right thing but your bodies are weak.

James extinguishes the 4th candle, and falls back to sleep.

Reader 2: Jesus went away a second time and prayed:

Jesus: Father, if I must drink this cup, then I pray that what you want will be done.

Reader 1: Then he went back to his followers. Again, he found them dozing. So he let them sleep, and went away once more and prayed. Then went back to them again.

Jesus: Are you still dozing and snoring? The time has come for the Son of Man to be handed over. Stand up. We have to go. And here comes my friend to do the job.

Judas enters. John blows out the 5th candle.

Reader 2: Judas had a crowd with him, all carrying weapons. They had been sent from the priests and leaders. Judas had a plan to show them which one was Jesus.

Judas: The one I kiss is Jesus.

Reader 1: So Judas walked up to Jesus and kissed him on the cheek. Then the men seized Jesus and arrested him.

Judas extinguishes the 6th candle and leaves, followed by Peter, James, John and the other disciples.

Reader 2: The soldiers took Jesus into the governor's palace and put a purple robe on him and made a crown of thorns and stuck it on his head. They began chanting and laughing:

Everyone: Jesus, king of the Jews!

Reader 1: They kept on beating him and spitting on him. Then they knelt in front of him and pretended to honour him as a king. After they finished making fun of him, they took off the purple robe and gave him his own clothes to put back on. Then they gave him a heavy cross to carry, and took him outside the city to kill him.

Jesus extinguishes the last candle and is led out of the room.

From outside the room: the sound of nails being hammered into a piece of wood.

Reader 1 (over the sound of hammering):

> I hold the nail in my hand:
> rigid, sharp, unbending.
> You held the nail in your hand:
> split, torn, bleeding.

Christ of the nail,
you were hanging on for me,
aching for the end,
ready to expire.
How can I ever say
'It is finished'
and walk away? …

Silence

Reader 2:   Go out into the darkness.
Go out into the world.
Go out with Jesus Christ
into the night.

Folk leave in silence and darkness.

Readings based on:

Matthew 26:17–19, Invitation to the Passover meal
Matthew 26:20–23, Betrayer
Matthew 26:26–30, the Last Supper
Matthew 26:31–35, Jesus predicts Peter's denial
Matthew 26:36–41, Gethsemane
Matthew 26:42–46, The disciples still sleeping
Matthew 26:47–50
Mark 15:16–20

Note:

1. This liturgy is based on a process of retelling the Passion story with children and young people. This can involve re-reading written versions together and discussion. More than one retelling can arise. Some commonly held remembering can emerge. Whilst remembering the Bible is not necessarily about rote memory, this sometimes does get included. Individuals have different capacities for rote memory and some can remember a lot more than others. Even so, a

few commonly held words or phrases may stick in a remembered version. For example, remembering the Last Supper may include such key phrases as 'This is my body'. Such phrases do not belong to any specific translation but are truly part of the community corpus; they belong to us all, as they echo through our liturgies time and time again.

From time to time a specific translation may influence the remembering of a community. Again, this is a gift, to build up the body of Christ. Remembering the Bible together is the space where all these opportunities meet, and this liturgy is the product of such a process.

On a hill
An outdoor service for Good Friday

Bob Warwicker and Janet Lees

Guidelines for leaders:

This service is a compilation of some of the material we have used on Good Friday afternoons on a hill overlooking Huddersfield, in England, following a five-hour walk from an outlying area. (Not everyone does the walk!)

It's always better to share the reading, praying parts around. But the people who do this must have strong voices, even if using amplification; people will have to compete with the wind, dogs, etc.

If hymns are used, they must be in a style that suits the people most likely to attend and be familiar to them. If the singing is unaccompanied, it helps to identify someone musical who can start everyone on the right note. Much welly needs to be used!

Time: aim for 20 minutes overall, 25 maximum.

Adapt the material here to suit your setting and community. Use as much or as little as works for you.

Welcome:

Good afternoon, everyone, and welcome.
We are here to remember the death of Jesus on a hill outside the city.
Christians believe that his death was not the end.

But here and today we remember his suffering, his pain,
the way he was a victim of political violence,
and his love.

Opening prayer:

O God, we worship you this day.
We worship you on this day of death and destruction.
We worship you trusting still
in your love and forgiveness,
the love and forgiveness that we see in Jesus,
even in his dying breath,

when he was executed that day long ago
by people like us.

Bible readings:

Some examples of what we have used over the years:
Psalm 22:1–2, or 1–3, or 14–16a, or 1–2, 6–7, 11, 16–18, 20, 23–24
John 18:1–11
Isaiah 53:1a, 3–5

Hymn or song:

'There is a green hill far away' or 'The old rugged cross'

Prayer:

Living God,
on this day, we praise and worship you.
On this day, with the hills all around,
the sky above,
the grass beneath our feet,
we worship you,
our loving Creator.

Yes, this is a good place.
But it is hard to call this day,
this Good Friday,
it is hard to call this day good.
For this is a day of remembering.
It is a day of remembering
the terrible things we do to one another.

It is a day of remembering
the terrible things we do to you.

It is a day to remember how people like us,
and politicians like the ones we support,

brought Jesus to the place of shame and suffering,
and had him executed on a cross.

It's a day of remembering
that there's a bit of Pilate in each of us,
washing our hands,
keeping our noses clean.

There's a bit of the angry Barabbas in each of us.

There's a bit of Judas in each of us.

There's a bit of the High Priest, and the executioner, in each of us.

There's a bit of Peter's cowardice in each of us.

There are people like us in every vengeful crowd.

God, forgive us.
God, have mercy on us.
For we are human.
And we do wrong.
And today we cling to your promises,
your promise to forgive us
when we turn to you.
God, forgive us.

On this day, God, we cling to the cross,
that wooden contraption of death
from 2000 years ago,
that old rugged cross.

We hold tight to the cross,
and what it says about your love,
about your solidarity with human suffering,
about our wrongdoing and your forgiveness,
about depths of meaning far beyond what we can express.

On this day, this Good Friday,
God of love,
we worship you.

And/or:

Living God,
as we meet to remember
how Jesus was executed on a cross,
we confess that we are sorry for this cruel world.

We are sorry that we have allowed the world
to become such a place,
where the innocent suffer
and your Son dies.
Your Son, Jesus Christ,
who came to show us love,
who came to bring healing,
who came to speak the truth to power,
who came to offer peace,
who dies because of
the cruel necessities of politics.

God forgive us, we pray.
God forgive us our complicity
in such a world that still exists today.
Father God, give us a penitent spirit
as we learn again of the suffering of Jesus,
as we learn again
of the hope you offer.

And/or:

Living God,
as we meet to worship you today,
we see the whole town spread out below us:
with all its suffering and hope,
its work and redundancy,
its violence and peace.

God, help us today
to bring together our thoughts of this town
with our thoughts of Christ,

remembering how he was crucified
outside the gates of Jerusalem …

Bible reading:

For instance: Mark 15:16–32

Reflection:

We are the cross people.

Today we are the cross people.

For more than two thousand years this hill has been a place of human life.

For more than _____ years, on Good Friday, this hill has been a place of remembering: remembering the story of the hill far away and the Suffering One.

Today we are the cross people.

We have come from east and west and north and south to this hill.

We have come cross-wise through the cross-woods, along the cross-paths, by the cross-streets, past the cross-roads.

We have come to remember the cross-hill.

Today we are the cross people.

On this liminal day, we have trod the path between life and death, to hear the story of the cross, to keep the vigil, to remember.

We are the Good Friday people, bringing here in our lives, in our memories, in our prayers, all the thoughts and stories and hope of the cross-people of our day: the people who tread the path between life and death around the world in *(topical examples …)*.

As we remember the cry of the Crucified One: 'Father, forgive', we ask God's forgiveness for the forgetting, for the ignoring, for the rejecting, of those for whom we pray today.

As we remember the Tortured One, we pray for all those who face unjust trials today.

As we remember the Insulted One, we remember those who are united with him today.

May we, the cross people, bear his story in our lives as we leave the cross-hill and return to the world of the Three-Day Mystery, ready to be his witnesses.

Bible reading: Isaiah 52:13–53:10

Reflection: A perversion of justice

Don't say it was all a plan.

Don't say that in some distant ivory-tower salon of cruelty, God devised the savage death of Jesus as the route to salvation for the human race.

No, think again about Good Friday.

Something deeply dirty was done that day.

The death of Jesus was all wrong.

It wasn't God that killed Jesus, it was the Roman Empire.

And the Roman Empire was behaving like other empires, before and since.

The Roman people, their governors and soldiers, and the fastidious and inhumane religious authorities, and the friends who deserted Jesus, they were all behaving like people do.

But ...

But can we believe that God can rescue meaning out of the most messy, horrible and devastating situations?

The meaning of Good Friday is that God stays with us.

The message of this day is that Jesus has been there too.

Jesus is there now, with you in that struggle.

You can place your hand in his hand.

This is how Good Friday ends, not with a blaze of dawn light; that is for another day.

Good Friday ends in pain and darkness.

But it is a pain, it is a darkness inhabited by the God of love.

Song: 'Were you there when they crucified my Lord?'

After this hymn, ask people to imagine being at Jesus' crucifixion as:

Pilate …
A religious leader …
The Emperor …
Someone in the crowd …

So it's come to this, has it, Jesus?
No one to stand by you now, not in this
God-forsaken hour.
For human contact, only raw hammer blows.
Maybe we could understand
the tearing wrists, the straining lungs,
but who could comprehend the weight of transgressions you feel?
Herod's murderings *(list of current horrors in the world …)*
meeting in your body.

Each little cruel word spoken by a husband or a wife,
a parent or a child.

Every scream in the dark,
every unseen battering.

This is the cup you drink,
and no one to share with you.

No one to stand by you, Jesus, in this time.

Yet, in this time, for all time, you stand by us:
you drink the cup of our sorrow.

Hymn or song

Prayer:

Topical prayers of intercession, and:

God bless *(name of town)*.
Guide its people and keep them safe.
Where there is stress, bring healing.
Where there is enmity, bring peace.
Where jobs are in danger, bring security.
Where people work too hard, bring rest.

Let your faith fill this town.
Let your hope inspire this town.
Let your love enfold this town.
God bless *(name of town)*.

The Lord's Prayer (said together)

Hymn or song: 'When I survey the wondrous cross'

The Grace (said together)

Blessing:

May God bless you on the journey.
If the load is heavy, may it not break you.
If the path is steep, may you not fall.
If you are tired, may you find rest.
If you have far to go, may a friend greet you at the end.

Drink this cup
A reflection and meditation

Stephen G Wright

Bible readings:

Luke 22:20; Matthew 26:39

Reflection:

This 73-year-old body of mine has been to as many countries, yet 40 of those years has included returns to Iona, and there is never a time when my heart does not take a little leap as the ferry leaves Fionnphort and I look out across the Sound to the island and the Abbey.

I left the mainland during the pandemic, in a brief interlude between lockdowns, knowing there were two good friends each in their own way facing great suffering, one of them in intensive care with Covid-19, the other with cancer. I heard the same from both of these people as I have heard from hundreds of others down the years of my time as a spiritual director. 'I'm good with this.'

I've lost count of the number of times that someone who has passed through great suffering – abuse, violence, public shame, poverty, disease, bereavement – has said quietly, almost conspiratorially, different versions of the same theme: 'I can say this to you, because I know you will understand, though I could never say it to some people, that a part of me is grateful for this (disease, trauma …), because without it I would not have changed to know the wholeness, the wonder I know now.' In suffering there is always, somewhere, a grace, albeit a fierce one, that is an offering for transformation and getting closer to the Beloved.

I also carried with me, as I walked up the road to the abbey, all the commentary about 'this terrible virus' and its effects, from the tragedies of deaths to the trivia of complaints of cancelled holidays or shopping inconvenience.

As I got closer to the abbey, there was an almost post-apocalyptic sense of neglect, like in those films of dystopian futures where we see cities in decay after the people have disappeared. Here, with the absence of the work of its caretakers, the place had taken on an air of ruinous reversion. And the words of the prayer attributed to St Columba came to mind: *'Ere the world ends, Iona will be as it was.'* Was this a glimpse of that time to come when all that people have built gradually returns to nature, which, if left long enough, would leave it as if we had never been here?

The cloisters were layered with guano, rabbits scattered into the foundations, grass grew knee-high where once there were neat lawns. Unusually large flocks of sparrows fed on the grassheads of sparrow heaven. Broken gates gave them perches. Damp, unrestrained, was taking over the crafted stones. The empty abbey, cleared of movable furnishings, had a mournful echo. Dust and detritus were everywhere. Weeds crept in over once well-trod paths. The Street of the Dead was grass-grown, the cobbles lost beneath it.

And thus it was – with the voices of others speaking about these dark times ringing in my ears and the voices in myself pitying the scene of disorder all around me – that I went to the abbey for a time of solitude and guidance, as has long been my habit on arrival. Even though the island hotels had recently reopened for business, visitors to Iona were few. On a peak-tourist, high-summer day, I had the abbey as my own vast private chapel.

I knelt before the altar. And one of those moments of magical synchronicity charged in as, for some unaccountable reason, only three of the words on that great marble slab were clearly illuminated. Of course my rational mind told me that it was the effect of the dust, or because of the angle of the afternoon sun or my position on the cold floor … but my rational mind had no purchase here. I just saw those words; then it seems I heard them more deeply than ever before. The journey here indeed seemed a preparation of receptivity for them. 'Drink this cup …'

My thoughts tumbled around the things in my own life, in my own body, that were causing suffering that 'I do not want' … matched by the words of millions in the media, the voices national and international all speaking of 'these bleak times'. Such is our inclination to dualism, a world where light and dark must be separate. It seems naturally right to want the 'bad stuff' to go away and want only bliss and joy and peace to hang around. It seems counter-intuitive, indeed perverse, to suggest otherwise. The poet Rumi sang *'Oh break my heart, oh break my heart, oh break my heart again'* … His longing for God was so great that he was willing to shed all presuppositions of self and attachments that he might break free of the grip of the earthly realm of time and space and unite with the Beloved while still in it. 'Break my heart?'

– who on earth would want that? Yet it is interesting to note that so many words in the spiritual life are fierce ones when it comes to the deepening of faith and our longing for the Beloved. From the earliest times Christian contemplatives have peppered their writings with: *'surrender'* (Augustine), *'drowned and liquefied in an unknown darkness'* (van Ruysbroeck), *'consumed by divine fire'* (Hilton), *'annihilation'* (Benet). That is not to say that in 'Thy will be done' this is a Divine who demands suffering or that we have to suffer in order to Come Home. Rather, it is about a willingness to embrace the fullness of what it is to be human, and to know that the suffering I-who-think-I-am is not the only I that I Am. The soul is having a human journey – the former is timeless, the latter will end.

And yet those words, 'Drink this cup' – this cup of life, all of life ... Nowhere does Jesus tell us that by following him (and he does tell us to follow him, Matt 4:19) that everything in life will be tickety-boo thereafter. Quite the contrary. Look where following leads him. To that second request of the cup, knowing the immense suffering that was about to face him, in his humanity he asks for it to be taken from him ... yet realises the futility of that and has only one response: 'Thy will be done.'

To drink the cup of life is to drink all of it – there is no suggestion that this drink is all sweetness and light, nothing in the small print that says if you drink it you will never know pain and grief again. Indeed the suffering may be heightened as, with the awareness and love of the Absolute, we may see more deeply just how things might be if we were all fully awakened. Such an awakening to equanimity does not lead us to passive detachment however, rather to an engaged compassionate action, but within defined limits. 'Thy will not mine' – all our actions can be discerned as healthy or unhealthy according to whether we follow our will or the Beloved's will. With Love and awareness we are better able to embrace life in all its pain and bliss, neither pushing away the former nor grasping at the latter, and act with greater equanimity.

There is a story from the Christian contemplative tradition. Jesus, on his way to Jerusalem, encounters a group of people who are full of anguish and fear. He asks them why this is so. They reply, 'Master, we have spent our lives trying to avoid suffering, yet still it comes to us.' He blesses them and walks on.

Then he meets another group, similarly anguished, and asks them why this is so. 'Master,' they reply, 'we have spent our lives trying to be only happy and joyful, and still suffering has befallen us.' He blesses them and walks on.

Then he meets a third group, whose faces are etched with the lines of both joy and suffering in life, yet who radiate a tranquil air. He asks why this is so. 'Master,' they respond, 'we gave up trying to always get happiness or striving to avoid suffering.' 'Truly,' he says, 'you have found the way to the Kingdom of Heaven.' And he blesses them and walks on to the city and to his fate.

Meditation:

How far have you been able to drink the bittersweet cup of life? Are you able to drink in full remembrance – re-membering, joining again – of your relationship in Christ and all that it entails, compassion and service, suffering and death, with acceptance and harmony?

Or do you judge things around you, and in yourself, as 'good' or 'bad', desirable or undesirable?

Do you strive to enjoy only happy and rewarding times, and make great effort to avoid the sad and the challenging?

How far have you been able to drink of the cup of life, all of it, and find in it redemption and repentance (the latter in the true sense of metanoia: changing your way of being, as opposed to asking forgiveness for 'sins') and a great equanimity, no matter what arises?

Birth and death, creation and destruction are part of life; that which is built up falls down, everything is time-bound in the temporal realm. Are you able to accept that fully while knowing when and where to apply your energies, when to let go, when to act?

How deep is your faith, your trust, in the Beloved? At some unfathomable level, outside of the temporal and in the eternal, do you believe, in the words of Mother Julian, that *'All shall be well, and all manner of thing shall be well.'*?

Sit with all these questions before the altar of your relationship with the Beloved; be open to insight, challenge and wisdom with whatever it is time for you now to receive …

On the other side of this day
A reflection for Holy Saturday

John Murning

I have conducted a lot of funerals over the years:
funerals where people have died
in car accidents and house fires;
funerals where people have died tragically
as a result of a freak accident;
funerals where people have taken their own life;
funerals where folk have lived to a very old age;
and funerals of stillborn babies.
I have conducted funerals of those who have died suddenly
with massive heart attacks
and funerals of those who have suffered for many years
with terminal illnesses.
There have been funerals of folk who spent time in prison,
and funerals of those who have been honoured by the Queen
for their service to the country.
Some of these funerals have been grand affairs
with horse-drawn carriages, marching bands or lone pipers,
and on one occasion, a motorbike cavalcade for a biker funeral.

The saddest of funerals are always those where it is just
me, the undertakers and the gravediggers.
National Assistance funerals they call them now;
previously they were known as paupers' funerals.
Quite often at such events
the only thing I am likely to know about the person
is their name, and perhaps their age.
I know not if they had any family, or even children,
and if anyone turns up who has known them
they will often stand at a distance
as though they were just passers-by.
Sometimes families just cannot afford the funeral costs,
and so don't even claim the body,
as it will then become their responsibility
to provide a suitable funeral service.
Often, they are laid to rest
in a separate area of the graveyard
in what used to be called the paupers' graveyard:

a wee bit of land laid aside by the local authority
for those who have no family, friends or money,
so that at the end of life the person can have some dignity,
and be laid to rest for all eternity.

Surprisingly, for one so popular,
only two people seem to participate in the burial of Jesus.
No parents, brothers or sisters or uncles!
None of the disciples
with whom he had spent the last three years of his life.
None of them wanted to take a risk
to turn up and honour him …
not because of the cost,
but for fear they would be identified as a follower,
and likely undergo the same fate as their Master.
Neither did any of the folk whom he
healed, or fed, or set free from bondage
make the effort to watch from afar.
Not a single person turned up to say goodbye.
Only Joseph of Arimathea,
a well-known and respected Jew,
and Nicodemus, who came with spices to anoint his body,
bothered to turn up to lay Jesus to rest with dignity.
Of course, it turns out to be a borrowed tomb,
maybe a temporary measure, until the family can do their own thing,
but it suggests that the Jesus movement is well and truly dead.
The followers are shattered and in hiding,
fearful that they might be next to be crucified,
and those who had hoped the Messiah would take power
are reminded that such things come at a price,
the price of spilled blood,
of the leaders and organisers.

So why are we here this morning?
Have we come to attend the funeral of Jesus,
to lay his body to rest, pay our last respects
and then get back on with our own lives?

Or have we come in the knowledge that this is just a moment in time,
a reminder of what the world could be like
without Jesus, and God, and the Holy Spirit in our lives?
An empty, barren, lonely, scary world.

And there will be moments in our faith journey
when we will feel this loss,
this loneliness, this barrenness.
Times when we will experience the darkness,
the numbness, the grief and despair of all that life can throw at us,
and where we know for real the sense of emptiness that loss brings.

Yet, here is what matters!
We know on the other side of this day
that there is hope, life and a future.
We know that there is always life
even in the midst of death,
and we must see that, live that,
and build the kingdom of God around life rather than around death.

Today we pause, and know darkness,
but tomorrow the light shines
and hope springs eternal.

Let there be light
Resources for Easter Day

Rodney Aist

I. Scripture readings

Then God said, 'Let there be light'; and there was light. And God saw that the light was good; and God separated the light from the darkness. God called the light Day, and the darkness he called Night. And there was evening and there was morning, the first day.

Genesis 1:3–5 (NRSV)

But on the first day of the week, at early dawn, they [Mary Magdalene and the other women] came to the tomb, taking the spices that they had prepared.

Luke 24:1 (NRSV)

In the beginning was the Word, and the Word was with God, and the Word was God … All things came into being through him, and … what has come into being in him was life, and the life was the light of all people. The light shines in the darkness, and the darkness did not overcome it.

John 1:1, 3–5 (NRSV)

II. Responsive reading

Leader: Christ is risen!
People: Christ is risen indeed!

Leader: Easter begins with a journey at early dawn
to anoint a crucified corpse.
People: It continues for eternity
with the whispered words of God's sovereign love:

All: Let there be light! Let there be life!
Leader: Christ is risen!
People: Christ is risen indeed!

III. Reflection

Let there be light!

Easter begins with a journey at early dawn to anoint a crucified corpse. It continues for eternity with the whispered words of God's sovereign love: 'Let there be light!' Resurrection is sparked by God, kindled by Christ and illuminated by the Holy Spirit.

Fire and sunlight are central to our Easter celebrations. Bonfires are stoked; paschal candles are lit. Sunrise services commence at dawn. Holy fire emerges from the tomb.

Easter is not the only festival that evokes the image of light, sunlight, candles and fire. There's the winter and summer solstice, Christmas and Candlemas, which, in some Christian traditions, is a day for blessing candles that are used throughout the year. Also known as the Presentation of Christ at the Temple, Candlemas falls forty days after Christmas, on February 2nd.

In the United States and Canada, sunlight and the 2nd of February also converge in Groundhog Day, which, in a twist, does not welcome the sun. If the groundhog sees its shadow, then spring is still far away.

In a world that often feels more winter than spring, full of hoarfrost instead of blossoms, we might be excused, amidst the Easter hallelujahs, if, confusing the festivals, we thought Jesus saw his shadow this morning and went back inside his tomb. Six more weeks, says the groundhog. Back inside his den. Back inside our homes. We know the routine. Six more weeks of the harrowing of Hell, but even that could be extended.

Easter, in a fallen world, can feel like a mutated version of Groundhog Day. We've seen rays of hope before and have learned not to hope. It's not that we want resurrection to be delayed, but it just doesn't look like we're there yet.

Oh well, we'll persevere. We're used to it by now – living in the meantime, betwixt and between – or so we say. But when extraordinary times are worse than ordinary ones, when the 'new normal' is not so normal, when we long to return to a recent past that itself was a place of longing, God knows, we could use a good resurrection.

If Jesus saw his shadow and returned to his tomb, at least we know where he is. And a sealed tomb is a cocoon of potentiality – though we only know that if we've already lived the story. If we, like Mary Magdalene and the other women, have ever been up on the first day of the week – when the dawn was still dark, off to anoint the bodies of our broken dreams – then maybe we know something about the surprise of resurrection.

Maybe we know that this is how Easter happens. God's word interrupts the silence. Day breaks from the darkness. Light emerges and remains, and we didn't see it coming.

The resurrection of Christ reactualises the first day of creation, when God spoke, 'Let there be light.' Easter is the inception of creation as much as the culmination of crucifixion. It's the beginning not the ending. Easter is the genesis of the Christian life: light appears in the darkness, and the darkness has not overcome it.

Easter occurred on a Sunday, but since we celebrate the day of the Resurrection as a holy day, we lose some of its original context – Easter happened on the first day of the week. Easter, in other words, was a weekday, workday event. It's as if we're accompanying Mary Magdalene to the tomb on Monday morning. To grasp the impact of the resurrection story – how God transforms the chaos of the world into an everyday sanctuary of time – we should envision Easter Sunday as Monday morning.

Sundays come easily; Mondays are a different state of mind. If Sunday is a holy day, Mondays are the blues.

A school shooting in the United States occurred on a Monday in 1979, perpetrated by a sixteen-year-old student. When asked why she committed such a horrible crime, her response was dark and dreich: she hated Mondays. The story inspired the song 'I don't like Mondays' by the Irish band the Boomtown Rats, which became a number one single in the UK.

Mondays are days of fatigue, rust, regret, anxiety and trepidation, a point more comically made by Garfield, the cartoon cat, whose hatred for Mondays is his personal mantra.

On Mondays, the immediacy of the weekend lingers. There's a rear-view quality to Mondays. Just ask Mary, whose mind that morn was on the crucifixion. Mondays, above all, catch us unprepared.

To arrive at the Resurrection, we should take a Monday approach to the tomb. As we venture into the world unprepared, having no hope and without God in the world (Ephesians 2:12), Easter is a weekday, everyday surprise.

I worshipped one Easter at the Korean Mission Church, an English-speaking congregation of international migrant workers on the outskirts of Seoul. Located on the third floor of an office building, the walls of the makeshift sanctuary were covered with paper cutouts proclaiming 'God is Alive'. People sat in folding chairs, crowding as close as they could to the front of the comfortably packed hall. An adjacent room contained beds for overnight guests – abuse victims, displaced migrants and homeless individuals.

When visitors were introduced, I shared these thoughts with the congregation: Mary Magdalene saw the risen Christ through her tears. The Resurrection happened on a workday. God is a God of surprises. Easter sets light to the world, and darkness can never overcome it.

That Easter, in the Korean Mission Church, Jesus didn't see his shadow. Rather, the tomb was cleared out; winter was over. The risen Christ was with them – there among second-place people far from home, poor and marginalised, hardworking yet joyful, courageous and faithful, representing lands and languages from around the world, bonded together by their hope in Christ. While Cleopas was still on his way to Emmaus (Luke 24), there in Seoul, worship transitioned into lunch, before the tables were cleared for studies, games and English lessons.

On Monday morning, at early dawn, church members would set out again to the factories or to jobs of caretaking and cleaning, still others to work the markets, seeking a living, if not a better life. In a world that often feels more crucified than resurrected, Easter is the word of life that God speaks into our hearts. In a world full of planetary darkness, Easter is the light of God in the world.

That Easter, in the Korean Mission Church, Jesus didn't see his shadow. Not that clouds blocked the sun, but light casts no shadow upon itself. Jesus didn't see his shadow, because Christ himself is the light, a light which transcends the beginning of time.

At the same time, Easter returns us to the first day of creation, to an additional light that God spoke into being. According to Abraham Joshua Heschel, the light created on the first day, which was different from the sun, illuminated the world from end to end, but since we were unworthy of such light, God concealed it from our sight. For Heschel, something of that light appears on the sabbath, the seventh day, as *'spectral glimpses of eternity'*.[1] That, no doubt, is the case. But the light spoken into being at the dawn of creation occurred on the first day, which, for Christians, is the day of resurrection.

Two lights, therefore, converge on Easter. The divine light of Christ and the expansive light of God's creation. Together, they cast no shadows but illuminate the world from one end to the other. Light begets light. Easter heralds eternity.

Resurrection is God's response to darkness and chaos, to death and destruction, to the worst of what can happen. Resurrection occurs in our homes and on our way to work, in the brightness of Sunday dawn and in the darkness of Monday morn. Easter is the beginning not the ending. It's the genesis we didn't see coming. The first of many days to come.

Easter begins with a journey at early dawn to anoint a crucified corpse; it continues for eternity with the whispered words of God: 'Let there be light!'

Christ is risen! Christ is risen indeed!

Christ is alive! Hallelujah! Amen.

IV. Prayer

God of light, light before darkness, light before time, our journey to the tomb arrives in the darkness of dawn, in the still silence of chaos, in the shattered realisation that nothing has changed. On our journey to anoint a crucified corpse, we see the emergent shadows of yet another day.

In a world that often feels more winter than spring, we've seen rays of hope before and have learned not to hope. And, thus, we are deaf to your whispered words of sovereign love: 'Let there be light! Let there be life! Let us begin again.'

You surprise our clandestine journeys with the surprise of resurrection. Your word interrupts the silence. Light emerges and remains, and we didn't see it coming. You surprise our weekday journeys with everlasting life. You breathe life into our flesh. Love emerges and remains, and we didn't see it coming.

When our mind is on crucifixion, resurrection catches us unprepared. When life has been sealed with despair, you roll the stone away.

You transform the chaos of crucifixion into the cosmos of creation. Easter is the genesis we struggle to imagine. It's the inception of creation, the reception of life. Resurrection, you remind us, is the beginning not the ending. Christ's resurrection is the beginning of our week, the beginning of our work, the beginning of our lives.

In a world that often feels more crucified than resurrected, Easter is our commencement – you speak the word of life into our hearts. In a world full of darkened shadows, Easter is our illumination – you are the light of the world.

We stand before you in the quarried garden of resurrection haze. We are solemn but giddy, grateful but woozy, uncertain but certain. Is it you, really you? If so, say our names again! Jesus, the unexpected gardener, replies: 'Mary, Mary, don't be afraid!'

You journey with us, risen Christ, from tomb to town, bringing resurrection into our homes, our lives and our relationships. Resurrection happens on our way to work, as we study, as we play, in our streets, markets and neighbourhoods, near and far, around the world, in the brightness of Sunday dawn and in the darkness of Monday morn. Easter is the beginning not the ending. The first of many days to come.

When the worst has happened, resurrection is spoken: 'Let there be light; let there be life.' The light of Christ shines in the darkness, and the darkness cannot overcome it.

Christ, kindle your light within us so that we, too, may be your resurrection light in the world.

We offer this prayer in the illuminating power of the Creator, the Redeemer and the Holy Spirit. Happy Easter, Holy Easter – Christ is alive!

Amen.

Sources and acknowledgements:

1. *The Sabbath*, by Abraham Joshua Heschel, Farrar, Straus and Giroux, 2005, p.36

New Revised Standard Version Bible, copyright © 1989 the Division of Christian Education of the National Council of the Churches of Christ in the United States of America. Used by permission. All rights reserved.

Easter morning at the Split Rock

Jan Sutch Pickard

Introduction:

This Eastertide resource for individual reflection or group worship is inspired by a particular place, a landmark on the Isle of Mull. Of course, it isn't tied to that place. Like much other worship material, it could be adapted, with the readings and prayers here being used in other locations, indoors and out, online or in a recorded service.

However, setting the scene can also help.

Fionnphort is a little ferry port at the far western end of the Ross of Mull. The island of Iona, destination of tourists and pilgrims, is just half a mile away, across the Sound of Iona. Folk living or staying on Iona have the opportunity to trace the events of Holy Week 'in real time'. But from Mull it is only possible to join in the sequence of services when the ferries are running. For the rest of the time, as for the rest of God's children, the challenge and invitation is to worship where we are, and with our neighbours.

Usually there will be a crowd catching the morning ferry for the big Easter Morning celebration in the Abbey on Iona. But if people on Mull want to hold an Easter Dawn service, it will need to be on home ground – just as Christians in many other places seek a hilltop or garden, sometimes even a graveyard, to remember the first encounters with the empty tomb and risen Christ. For some years now, a great boulder on Fionnphort beach, or a spot overlooking it, has been a focus for a service early on Easter Day, taking a different form each time.

The service offered here has been prepared by someone who has worshipped there with their neighbours, sometimes leading, always blessed by the simplicity and sense of God's Spirit present, outside the walls of the church and here and now.

Music suggested for this service:

On Easter morning it's good to sing!

Therefore a number of hymns or short choruses are suggested. Even if this isn't public worship, but personal devotion, you may find these tunes resounding in your head.

'Morning has broken' (to *Bunessan*) is a well-known hymn that has been sung year after year on the shore here. Eleanor Farjeon's words are a simple expression of joy in God's constantly re-created world – and the Resurrection – set to a traditional Gaelic air, which is named after a village on the Ross of Mull.

'The Lord's my Shepherd' (to *Crimond*) is appropriate because the story starts at the tomb and this setting of Psalm 23 has given solace to many in a time of bereavement. Next to the beach where the Split Rock lies is the village graveyard, where for centuries unaccompanied singing of this psalm might have been heard.

'Love endures/Jesus Christ is risen today ...' (to *Easter hymn*) belongs to a wider tradition: a 14th-century Latin hymn, found in an 18th-century collection, *Lyra Davidica*, with words later written by Charles Wesley, then adopted and adapted by different denominations. The fourfold Alleluia included in each verse is a reminder of the Catholic tradition that, not sung at all during Lent, this acclamation bursts out joyfully on Easter Sunday. The tune most often used for it – *Easter Hymn* – can be found on the Internet or, for example, in the Church Hymnary 4 (410).

The *'Iona Gloria'* – according to tradition – was sung by the monks as they rowed to and fro across the Sound of Iona.

A *'Kyrie'* could be sung. No particular setting is suggested here, but if this is a musical tradition that you value, you may at this point be using music from a different part of the world – like Ukraine. The Easter story is universal.

Responses:

Early in the morning we gather:
Longing for meaning.

As the world wakes up, once more:
Aware of so much brokenness.

Between the graveyard and the cracked boulder:
Looking for signs of God's presence.

In the sound of the waves, the song of a bird:
Hoping to hear God's voice.

In this time and place, together and alone:
Yearning for new life.

Song: 'Morning has broken' (to the tune *Bunessan*), or 'Psalm 23' (to *Crimond*)

Prayer:

God of love and life,
there are times when we feel that we have lost you,
that you have gone far away, out of reach:
as we stand by a hospital bed,
sit in a lonely home, separated from family;
as we struggle with growing gaps of memory,
watch someone we love suffering,
when the world news makes us despair;
standing at the foot of the cross,
in a frosty garden, by a graveside,
on a cold shore, among the world's waste,
we grieve your absence, our loss.

And yet you have not gone away,
you are there mysteriously,
even in the darkest places,
even when they – and we – feel empty.
There, most of all, you are present:
you are there for us.
In Jesus you lived and died as God-with-us, Immanuel.
And you came back to life, in our lives.

Out of death's silence you speak a living Word.
Speak to us and through us, now,
living, loving God.
Amen

Reading (1): Luke 23:55–24:2

Narrator: Here we stand, in imagination (if we were present in reality we might have wet feet) gazing at a great rock which the ice sheet aeons ago scraped from a mountain, carried in its slow flow and set down in a strange place, on a beach, on the edge of an island. It's a good place to come on Easter morning to reflect on a story from long ago and far away. In the story, women – the least powerful members of a community living on the edge – have come to a graveyard, bereaved, and are staring with a mixture of grief and disbelief at a stone that has been rolled away from the mouth of a tomb. What are they to make of it? And where is the body of their friend? Where is the one they have come to mourn? How can they make sense of this?

Folk living on the Ross of Mull gather at this rock on Fionnphort beach on Easter Morning. Between the village graveyard and the ferry slipway, below the busy street with buses, shop and pub, passed daily by many, on pilgrimage or more mundane journeys to Iona. Some think it looks like a giant Easter egg – cracked open! Others see – in the way it has been almost cleft in two – a symbol of Christ's resurrection, the setting-free of the Spirit into the world.

Local history records that the granite rock, which had long been a landmark on this beach, was split by quarrymen who had a use for it – but before they could finish the job and cart it away, geologists told them to desist, for this is a fine example of an erratic boulder.

Prayer:

God of constant creation,
a changing universe,
help us to value those things around us
that we cannot explain.
Teach us to explore and question
before we exploit the natural world.
Help us not to be afraid of what we cannot understand,
to witness where your Spirit is being set free.
Bless us with wonder
and the belief that you are present
in every aspect of our lives.
Amen

Reading (2): Luke 24:3–9

Song: 'Love endures' (to *Easter hymn*), or 'Iona Gloria'

Love endures (Luke version)

The storytelling version here was developed in all-age services on the Isle of Ulva.

Jesus Christ is risen today, Alleluia,
Our triumphant holy day, Alleluia.
Who did once, upon the cross, Alleluia,
Suffer to redeem our loss, Alleluia.

Women come at break of day, Alleluia,
Find the stone is rolled away, Alleluia.
In the garden gapes a cave, Alleluia,
Terror of an empty grave, Alleluia.

Dawn is dazzling them with glory, Alleluia,
Angels tell a joyful story, Alleluia.
Wondering women hear it said, Alleluia,
'Do not search among the dead – Alleluia,

Jesus lives!' The women run, Alleluia,
Trusted to tell everyone, Alleluia.
'Jesus lives!' the news they share, Alleluia,
Faith is stronger than despair, Alleluia.

Now let everything that lives, Alleluia,
Share the hope the Gospel gives, Alleluia.
Ring, you rocks, and sing, you shores, Alleluia,
Death's defeated, love endures, Alleluia.

Narrator: Luke's Gospel names the women who, according to this account, became the wondering witnesses and trusted messengers: Mary of Magdala, Joanna and Mary the mother of James. We're told that other women quickly became part of this mission to share the good news, taking it to the apostles first – and then, and then – where would it all end?

It could have ended right there. For, we are told, 'They were not believed.'

They were women, so legally their witness wasn't valid, and culturally, their experience was not valued. They were going to lay out the body – if they had touched it they would have been unclean. The women were outsiders to the authoritative group of the apostles.

Some versions of Luke add a verse where Peter goes to the tomb to see for himself, sees it empty and is amazed. But when the women described the same thing to the apostles, 'The story appeared to them to be nonsense.'

Reading (3): Luke 24:10–11

Song: 'Kyrie eleison'

Prayer:

God of deep mystery – and common sense –
we confess the way we dismiss with contempt
the lived experience of other people
as though it's of no value,
as though what we cannot understand isn't worth the effort.
We confess how easily influenced we are by prejudice
or by the shouting of social media:
ready to rubbish the deeply held beliefs
and principled actions
of people whose lives are different from our own.
We see how easy it is to claim
that what we don't want to hear is 'fake news'.

Kyrie (repeated)

Help us, God of discernment,
to distinguish between truth and lies;
help us, God of compassion,
to understand where our sisters and brothers
are hurting or doubting or hoping;
help us to listen with great care for the good news –
and then to act on it.
Break open our hard hearts, and set your Spirit free.

Kyrie (repeated)

We thank you, God,
that, in your mercy, you forgive us,
redeem our failings, use our uniqueness,

bless our brokenness,
enable us to become landmarks for others,
signs of your love.

Kyrie (repeated)

And so we pray for all who need those signs:
folk struggling to make sense of life
or trying to find who they are;
those who have lost their way;
or who thirst for living water;
those who hunger for bread or justice;
those who mourn – and whose loss is overlooked;
those who glimpse hope –
but whose word is not believed.
Amen

Song: 'Morning has broken' (to *Bunessan*), or reprise 'Iona Gloria'

Blessing:

May God bless you where you are now,
and when you journey on to where you are called to be:
a place that will change you,
and where you can make a difference,
where you may be a sign of God's love
as you live out the Good News.
Amen

A wake-up call
A hymn for the Earth

Tom Gordon

This hymn was written for COP26, and can be used in any service of worship in which environmental concerns are the theme. It was originally set to the tune 'Sursum Corda', but it works equally well with 'Chilton Foliat', depending on the mood that's to be created in worship. Other 10 10 10 10 melodies might also be appropriate.

A wake-up call

The world is made by your creative hand.
You made us stewards of sky, and sea, and land.
And yet with carelessness or cruel design
we've wrought so much destruction over time.

We've caused the trees to burn, the seas to rise,
dispersed our carbon clouds throughout the skies,
plundered the earth for all that we could gain
and treated warning voices with disdain.

We took the greens, and blues, and vibrant reds,
and made them turn to black and greys instead.
We took the forests and abundant seas,
and then misused their riches as we pleased.

Forgive us now for every sin and shame.
For we should know we are the ones to blame.
Forgive us for the damage we have caused
by taking little heed of nature's laws.

For earth was given in trust to everyone,
to pass to generations yet to come.
So call us once again to work with you,
to give this fragile earth the care it's due.

And sound for us again a wake-up call –
that each of us should learn to give our all
to care for this, your world, in all we do,
and ever give abundant thanks to you.

I and the Other are one
Worship resources for Pentecost

Rodney Aist

I. Responsive reading:

Leader: Tongues of fire and the rush of violent wind.
People: Pentecost sends us out into the streets to engage the Other.

Leader: Filled with the Holy Spirit.
People: Pentecost is a life-changing encounter with the children of God.

Leader: Hearing God's voice in each our own language.
People: Pentecost speaks to God's passion for the particularities of human expression.

Leader: As a day of divine embrace.
All: Pentecost is God's insistence that I and the Other are one.

II. Reflection:

In the 1994 play *Pentecost*, by David Edgar, one of the characters tells a harrowing story about Serbian children being transported to the Jasenovac concentration camp during World War II. Wearing cardboard badges around their necks containing their personal information, the children, out of hunger, eat their nametags. The act signified a double death. Not only would the children die a physical death, no one would remember them, because, in their suffering, they consumed their identity. They ate their own history and, with it, their last trace of being.[1]

Pentecost calls us to remember. It calls us to remember how Christians have killed Christians and how Christians have killed the Other. It calls us to remember the unremembered, who, on our watch, have eaten their own names.

Pentecost marks the fiftieth day of Easter, and, with it, human agency has entered the Easter story. Easter is the celebration of eyewitnesses; Ascension is more of the same, but Pentecost gets us involved. If Easter locks us in an upper room and Ascension leaves us gobsmacked and uncertain of what to do, Pentecost sends us out into the streets to engage the Other. Receiving the Holy Spirit is more than a personal experience that warms our heart: it's a life-changing encounter with the children of God.

If Pentecost is the church's birthday – a common designation of the day – in what sense did Pentecost give birth to the church? To what did tongues of flame give labour? What gave its maiden cry when the rushing wind blew thither? The metaphor of birth speaks to a fundamental change in the Jesus movement that took place with the arrival of the Holy Spirit. The movement ceased to be a network of friends and related families. Following Jesus was no longer limited to the language and culture of the Galilean disciples. The Holy Spirit poured itself upon the nations of the world, men and women, young and old.

If by birthday, we mean a newfound identity that extends beyond our inner circle, then there's reason to cut the cake. We should be careful, though, to understand the story as a narrative of expansion rather than a breakaway event in the life of the church. To be touched by Pentecost is to speak universal truths of forgiveness, love and salvation, while holding sacred the cultural, ethnic and religious particularities of the Other.

As a day of divine embrace, as a celebration of expansive inclusion, Pentecost reminds us that, together with others, our lives are confirmed; our future is assured; our names are remembered.

By contrast, the harrowing image of the nameless children is the antithesis of Pentecost. While people spill out into the streets of Jerusalem, enraptured by the life-giving rush of the Holy Spirit, children endure the deadly enclosure of a boxcar train. While Pentecost confirms the future of the people of God, children eat their own history on their way to deaths without graves.

Social responsibility is both the blessing and the bane of the Christian life, and our failure to care for the Other turns the potentiality of Pentecost into a season of repentance. Instead of a double portion of the Spirit, the vulnerable suffer a double death. In place of pathways of life, a prelude to death derails the journey.

Christianity has always struggled to embrace the international reach of the Holy Spirit, far more than we're willing to admit. In times of conflict, Pentecost is one of the first biblical stories that we cast aside. Wars divide us into religious, ethnic and nationalist factions. Christians kill other Christians, Jews and Muslims, conquer and oppress indigenous people and demonise immigrants and refugees. Denominations and local churches struggle to recognise – let alone celebrate – the interpersonal diversity of the body of Christ, while issues of authority, power and privilege break along racial and ethnic lines.

By contrast, Pentecost people proclaim the universal reach of God; yet, we mustn't miss what Pentecost tells us about the way God works in the world – the principal takeaway of the Pentecost story is that God speaks to each of us in our own language. For the church to be the church, we must share God's passion for the particular, the sanctity of human diversity and the irreducible nature of personal experience.

To be the church in today's world, we must cease causing others to consume their names, denying their history, erasing their lives. Remember their names; say their names. Better yet, we must listen to their voices. Their history is our history; their future is ours. In listening to stories that are not our own, we hear the harmony of Pentecost. Their God is our God; our God is theirs. Pentecost is God's brazen insistence that I and the Other are one.

Pentecost is a Spirit-filled explosion of potentiality. One morning in Jerusalem, the Holy Spirit showed us the possibilities of what we could be – a church of the nations, experiencing God through the diversity of human expression. Sending us out into the streets, Pentecost calls us to transcend social boundaries, helping others to hear the voice of God.

Amidst the celebratory hymns, Pentecost is a day of repentance in which we confess that instead of speaking the language of others, we have silenced their voices and have erased their names. In the stark silence of suffering, Pentecost holds out hope that, in spite of our sins, God's children will be sustained by the physical and spiritual manna of the Holy Spirit. Over the cacophony of babbling tongues, Pentecost holds out hope that the names of the forgotten will be remembered.

If Pentecost is the birthday of the church, it's about becoming the children of God. If Pentecost is the birthday of the church, it's because we recognise God in the face of the Other and, in doing so, our sense of family has changed forever. Pentecost upsets who we thought we were; it changes our identity. Our world has expanded, which, in turn, makes the world smaller.

Pentecost is about God's universal presence in the particularity of human existence. As a day of divine embrace, as a celebration of God's expansive inclusion, Pentecost reminds us that, together with others, our lives are confirmed; our future is assured; our names are remembered.

Hearing God speak in our own language is God's confirmation that we are a part of the gospel story; hearing the gospel in our own language is God's insistence that we get it right.

The Pentecostal expanse of the Easter story sends us out into the streets to transcend the boundaries that divide us, to speak words that unite us, in the name of a God who overcomes death with life and darkness with tongues of fire, a God whom Peter reminds us will not abandon us to the realm of the dead. Children will be filled with the joy of God's presence, and God's holy ones will not see decay (Acts 2:27–28).

Our need for Pentecost is to save the Other from ourselves. The blessing of Pentecost is being forgiven by God, saved by Christ and renewed by the Holy Spirit. The surprise of Pentecost is hearing the Other say our name. Being spoken to, instead of speaking. Being spoken of, instead of forgotten. Salvation occurs when, coming full circle, we recognise God's voice in the Other and proclaim to the world that I and the Other are one.

III. Prayer of confession:

God of the gathered nations,
Christ of all people,
Spirit of divine embrace,

our failure to care for the Other turns the potentiality of Pentecost into a season of repentance. Instead of speaking the language of others, we have silenced their voices. Instead of celebrating the diversity of the body of Christ, we cling to homogenised identities, defining ourselves against the Other, denying the sanctity of human expressions that are not our own, failing to see beauty, let alone God, in the eyes of the stranger.

We spoil the party of Pentecost by wanting to have our cake and eat it too. Pentecost is a slice of the Spirit of God that we're unwilling to share.

Yet, there is no body of Christ without its members, no New Jerusalem without its nations, no us without the Other. Our rejection of your Pentecostal vision questions our place in the story, our identity as Easter people and the social implications of the empty tomb – our responsibility to care for the vulnerable, the dispossessed and disempowered, to see the cultural, religious and ethnic Other as the people of God.

In our cry for forgiveness, we confess that we have failed others through our deeds, misdeeds and inactions. In light of those we've harmed, we pray that the children of the world will be protected, the old honoured, the suffering relieved, the lowly exalted. Pour your Holy Spirit upon us, giving us a new identity that extends beyond the smallness of our world to the fullness of the family of God, and, being forgiven, let us hear, once again, stories of your love in our own language. Repeat your resurrection in our hearts, and descend once again into the depths of our soul, that we may look into the eyes of the Other and see the people of God.

In the Pentecostal power of the Holy Spirit. Amen.

Note:

1. *Pentecost*, David Edgar, Nick Hern Books, 1995, p.38

Wild Spirit
A prayer for Pentecost

Sandra Sears

Spirit of holy joy,
run wild
through us –
like a laughing child,
mouth wide open,
full of the wonder
of being alive.

Spirit of grieving anger,
blow wild
through bending branches.
Toss us out
of our nice, cosy nests,
to tumble and turn
in your raging currents.
Drive us out of complacency,
carry us into the unknown,
demand of us
dangerous choices.

Spirit of holy fire,
burn wild.
Destroy all that is dry,
lifeless –
dross that disguises
the pure beauty
of our true selves.

Spirit of life itself,
flow wild
through our veins,
wrap yourself around
our very bones,

thread yourself
through our DNA
so we no longer know
where we end
and you begin.

Wild, wild Spirit,
draw us into your dance,
your wild, wild dance
of love.

I walk with my father today
Worship resources for Father's Day

Tom Gordon

Like father

'Like father, like son,' they say.
'Like father, like daughter' too, I've heard.
But why?
Must I be defined by someone else,
someone 'they' think they know
so that they can identify in me something that's familiar,
something they assume they now know of me?
My build?
My smile?
My attitudes?
My faith?
My love?

Like father?
Perhaps …

Do I want to be 'Like father, like son'?
Yes, sometimes,
if being like him is about kindness, and calmness, and dependability.
I'd be happy with that,
and happy if people saw that in my own son too.

But do I want to be completely like him?
No, not ever,
if being like him is about snoring in his chair, drinking too much,
and not helping around the house.
I hope my son doesn't get these attributes from me.
And do I want only to be like him?
No, not at all.
For then I'd be a clone, a direct copy,
with nothing of myself, and everything from him –
and I don't want my son to be exactly like me!

So 'Like father, like son' is about taking the best,
and learning from the worst;
paying tribute to a source

and thanking God for a development;
accepting the 'nature' I've inherited,
and processing the 'nurture' I've received.

'Like father, like son,' they say.
Fine!
Though I would put it this way –

I like my father,
and I hope he likes how I've turned out too!

Father Tom

As a Presbyterian minister, I've been addressed in a variety of ways through the years. 'Minister' is common – even nicer as 'Meenister' in the Gaelic-influenced areas of Scotland. I'm familiar with 'The Reverend' or just 'Reverend', and, of course, 'Mr Gordon' might be a formal address or introduction. I once suggested to an elderly parishioner that she could call me 'Tom', to which she replied – with some vehemence, I should add – 'I'll do no such thing, laddie. For ye'll aye be Minister to me. Ah cannae be daein' wi' ower familiarity.' Though I chose not to point out that 'laddie' was, of itself, fairly over familiar – especially as it was being addressed to a thirty-five-year-old clergyman.

Only one person has ever addressed me as Father Tom.

Stephen was a patient in the hospice where I was chaplain. A devout Roman Catholic, he called me Father Tom the first time I met him. 'Thanks, Stephen,' I replied. 'But I'm not a Catholic priest. Tom, or Mr Gordon, or chaplain, or even padre, will be fine.' Stephen looked at me as if I was mad. 'You're a man o' the cloth,' he said. 'An' that means you're a Father to me. So, Father Tom it will be. OK?' And that's the way it was for the three weeks he was with us.

I gave Stephen Communion with three other patients. He was the only Roman Catholic, and when I reminded him that this wasn't a Mass, he smiled and said, 'It's the meaning that matters, no' how it's done.' Profound!

When Stephen was dying, he was in and out of consciousness. Since neither the Roman Catholic chaplain nor Stephen's parish priest were available, his nephew asked me if I would 'do the necessary' before he died. I assumed he meant prayers and an anointing, but I decided to give Stephen Communion. The Ward Sister was sceptical. 'He'll have no idea what's happening,' she said.

But when I placed a crumb of bread in Stephen's mouth and moistened his lips with a little wine on a sponge, Stephen opened his eyes. Struggling to focus, he eventually said, in a frail but distinct voice: 'Father Tom? Communion?' I nodded, held his hand, and said final prayers with him.

As he gently closed his eyes, I whispered, 'The Lord be with you, Stephen.' And a dying man replied, 'And also with you, Father Tom.'

Only one person has ever addressed me as Father Tom. But that has remained precious to me ever since. A Father to Stephen? Perhaps. Stephen as a Father ministering to me? You bet! And a loving Father for us both? You work it out.

My father

I learned from my father, my teacher, my guide.
His strength and his character can't be denied.
The ways he encouraged me; all he'd provide …
I learn from my father today.

I'm proud of my father, his character, poise;
his love for my mother, his time with his boys;
his long-lasting friendships, his loathing of noise …
I'm proud of my father today.

I've copied my father, and listened with care
to those who might need me awake and aware
to questions and probings … to be always there.
I copy my father today.

I feared for my father – mistakes that he made;
the times when his shouting could make me afraid;
his errors of judgment, when love was betrayed.
I fear for my father today.

I've measured my father – I have no complaint.
I can't make him out to be something he ain't!
A mixture, a muddle of sinner and saint?
I measure my father today.

I took from my father the lessons I've learned.
And when I remember, I'm always concerned
to glean from his life all the good I've discerned.
I take from my father today.

I've kept from my father what matters to me –
the traits that can make me what I need to be;
the flaws I'm aware of, and those I won't see …
I keep from my father today.

I've walked with my father – he's always around,
not safe in the heavens, or under the ground,
but here, in my life, with a presence profound.
I walk with my father today.

I'm thanking my father – I hope it's enough.
I'm trying to make sense out of all of the stuff
he's left me. And thinking about him is tough …
But I'm thanking my father,
I'm missing my father,
I'm needing my father,
I'm close to my father today.

The watch

Jodie has his father's watch. In truth, it wasn't his father's watch to start with. It was Jodie's. A gift, for Christmas, when he was seven. A gift from his father. A gift that he lost on Boxing Day.

That Christmas had been a strange one, twenty-two years ago. He learned later what he didn't know then, that his father had been made redundant from the Steel Mill in early December. He knew something wasn't right: the worried looks on his mother's face; his dad being at home when he wasn't usually; the gentle but constant reminders 'not to expect too much from Santa this year'. So why Jodie had gone on, and on, and on about the Lone Ranger watch he wanted for Christmas, he couldn't tell you – other than that he was seven, and it was Christmas, and that a Lone Ranger watch was the most important thing in the whole world.

Well, going on, and on, and on must have worn down the patience of his mum and dad, or been a major influence on Santa's generosity, but Christmas for the seven-year-old Jodie had been the best ever! For, on Christmas morning, he became the proud and excited owner of the longed-for Lone Ranger watch. And on Boxing Day he lost it!

He didn't exactly lose it. He knew where it was – somewhere between his back gate (where he knows it was on his wrist because he'd checked the time) and Mrs Cameron's garden on the other side of the village, where he'd gone to show his best friend, Zac, his Lone Ranger watch. But it wasn't where it should have been – on his skinny wrist. And that was the problem. His wrist was too thin for the watch to be fastened firmly in the last hole of the strap. His dad had said he'd punch another hole to make it tighter, if Jodie would leave the watch at home. But no! Jodie knew best. Zac had to see the watch. And, with skipping and tree-climbing, running and forgetting, the watch must have slipped off – somewhere between his back gate and Mrs Cameron's garden.

Oh, there was such a rumpus! There were tears – and not just from Jodie. There was being 'sent to bed for being careless'. There was a search party. There was a pall of gloom over what could have been the best Christmas ever.

The watch was found several days later. The whole village knew about the missing Lone Ranger watch. So, when it was discovered by a dog-walker a week after Christmas, it was returned from whence it had come. Well, not exactly, for it was returned to Jodie's father's pocket and not Jodie's wrist. For the watch was unusable and in a sorry state. It had sat in a puddle, and the watch-face was so cloudy you couldn't see the hands or the Lone Ranger or anything. Someone had stood on it and the glass was cracked. And it wouldn't go.

'What's the use of a watch that doesn't go?' was what Jodie's dad had said. 'What's the use' indeed? So, having shown Jodie the watch, it was returned to his father's pocket, and Jodie was left with an overwhelming sadness, and with his father's admonitions ringing in his ears: 'be more careful in the future'; 'save up and buy your own'; 'we don't have money to throw away'.

The Lone Ranger watch was never mentioned again. Jodie hadn't set eyes on it from that day – until now. For here it was, twenty-two years later, lying in Jodie's hand.

He'd discovered it amongst his father's 'stuff' in the top drawer of his desk. There was a clear-out to be done after Jodie's father's death – papers; artefacts; mementos; trivia; accumulated, meaningless junk – and a Lone Ranger that didn't have a cloudy or cracked face; that showed the Lone Ranger clear as day; and that was telling the exact time. It was in a brown, padded envelope, which contained a folded letter headed Time On Your Hands: Bespoke Jewellers and Watchmaker, and which read:

Dear Mr Cosgrove,

Please find enclosed your son's watch. It didn't take much repairing and I hope you'll find our work satisfactory. It was a pleasure to work on, and took me back to my own childhood when I had one exactly the same.

What a great idea to have it restored to its original condition for your son's 40th birthday. I'm sorry I haven't been able to source an original box. But I'm sure your son won't mind. As you said to me, he'll just be happy to have his watch back.

I hope he enjoys his birthday.

Best wishes,
James Allen, Watchmaker

PS

'Hi, ho, Silver. Away!'

Jodie has his father's watch. In truth, it wasn't his father's watch to start with. It was Jodie's. But then it wasn't his father's again, for twenty years. And now it was … Jodie's? No! It was his father's watch, made new, for him.

Jodie did, indeed, enjoy his 40th birthday, despite the sadness of his father not being around. That's why, in the afternoon, when he took his dog for a walk through the village, he kept checking his watch, not to find out the time, but to make sure his Lone Ranger watch was just where it should be – strapped to his wrist, always close to him, like his father would always be.

A prayer for Father's Day

Loving God,
we are to call you 'Heavenly Father',
'heavenly' because you're different,
divine, above, beyond,
too wonderful to comprehend;
and 'Father' because we can relate to that,
we know – or we think we know –
what fathers are about.

So we are bold to address you as 'Heavenly Father'
hoping that will be enough,
to revere you and know you,
at one and the same time;
ever holy, yet understandable by humanity;
ever mysterious, yet earthed in our lived experience.

Today we remember the fathers we know,
and use what we can relate to,
so we can understand the nature of God.

We give thanks for constancy,
and dependability, and familiarity.
We appreciate strength of character
and the provision of good things.
We value a father down on his knees in our world,
playing, cavorting, enjoying.

Thank you, Heavenly Father,
for your constant, unchanging love,
for your provision of all that is good,
for your Incarnate presence in our world.
We worry about the impatience of fathers,
and a lack of understanding.
We fear for a loud voice or
'just wait till your father gets home'.
We are distressed at absence when we needed presence,
for a lack of affirmation when we needed to be valued.

Come to us, Heavenly Father;
be patient with us when we do wrong;
scold us with a forgiving tolerance;
remind us of your presence when we fail to appreciate you.

We remember times of laughter and enjoyment,
and times of weeping and distress;
we remember the vigour of youth
and the wisdom of the passing years;
we remember the stories, old and new,
and the shared memories that have made stories for us.

Keep loving us, Heavenly Father;
raise up our joy and comfort our sorrow;
value our youthfulness and our experience of life;
teach us again the story of your love, and make it ever new.

Heavenly Father, we bring you our prayers,
thanking you for all fathers on this day,

grateful that in our gratitude for them
we can find windows being opened
from the human to the divine,
so that by remembering the 'father' part
we can find new insights into what is heavenly.

Amen

Holy space
A liturgy for St Benedict's Day (11th July)

Janet Lees

This liturgy is suitable for a wide range of ages and can be used by small groups or individuals.

Introduction:

'In response to the call of Christ, we seek to live holy communion, create holy space and offer holy service.' [1]

These are the words of the Promise made by members of the Lay Community of St Benedict, an ecumenical community *'dedicated to the Gospel and the spirituality of St Benedict as lived out by lay people'*.

The community gathers under the Rule of St Benedict, a spiritual guide written for monastics 1500 years ago in Italy.

The 73 chapters of the Rule are said to have been written so as not to be too difficult or hard. The themes of *holy communion, holy space* and *holy service* link to three key themes in the Rule: stability, hospitality and humility.

Opening responses:

Begin with prayer
And listen to the Holy Spirit.

Think about what you will say
And listen to the Holy Spirit.

Translate God's teaching into action
And listen to the Holy Spirit.

Prepare your heart and your body
And listen to the Holy Spirit.

Do not be intimidated or afraid.
Listen to the Holy Spirit.

(Based on words from the Prologue of the Rule of St Benedict)

HOLY SPACE

Spend some time thinking about what holy space means to you. If you wish, place something in the centre of the worship space to indicate these thoughts. It might be a photograph, a book, a plant, a stone, a shell, a CD … anything that conveys to you the notion of holy space.

Bible reading:

'A wise person builds a house on rock. Only foolish folk build on sand.'

From the Gospel of Matthew

Reflection:

St Benedict is remembered as the founder of Western monasticism. We recall the many monastic and basic Christian communities worldwide and their mission to represent Christ and to welcome the stranger in Christ's name. May our own spaces and places, homes and places of work, be like that too – open and welcoming. May we build on the rock of Christ who has stood as timeless witness to these ideals.

Prayer:

Cosmic-builder, bringing dust together, creating rock:
help us to found our lives on Christ,
the cornerstone that the builders rejected.
May our houses always stand open to friend and stranger,
to the homeless and the exiled,
so that everyone may find a home in you.

HOLY SERVICE

Spend a few moments thinking about what holy service means to you. Add something to the centre of the worship space that represents this to you. It might be something from your workplace – a laptop, a nurse's or supermarket worker's uniform; or something from home – a wash basin, a cooking pot; or something that signifies your faith commitment, or something else.

Bible reading:

'Listen and learn, young one: never forget what I teach you.'

Snippet from Proverbs 2

Reflection:

All of us are young ones when it comes to holy service: God can call us at any time to anything. Calling is not determined by age as we understand it.

Prayer:

God, may we listen and learn,
value and reflect all that you teach us,
and from deep within ourselves, create the holy space
that leads to holy service in your kindom.[2]

HOLY COMMUNION

Spend a little time thinking about what holy communion means to you. Place an item in the centre of the worship space that symbolises this to you: something that represents the community you belong to, or the way in which you are linked to other people: a badge, a logo, a photograph …

Bible reading:

'Lack of foods means even lions can get hungry:
But God ensures we lack nothing.'

Snippet from Psalm 34

Reflection:

Wildlife documentary programmes bring lions into our sitting rooms. We imagine the hungry lions with grumbling bellies, versus the fed lions with full tummies, sleeping their way through sunny afternoons.

Prayer:

God of hungry lions,
we thank you for our daily bread,
for your care that ensures we lack nothing.
Help us to feed and care for others.

Lord's Prayer:

In the form/language with which you are most comfortable.

Or use a version like this:

Holy One, always nurturing us,
we draw near,
mindful of the space and the grace:
may heaven and earth combine!
Feed us today, and forgive us
when we fail to feed others.
May we not be misled;
keep us on the right path,
travelling towards your kindom.

Prayer for going out:

'Always, we begin again.' (Rule of St Benedict)

It is the tradition in many faith communities to go directly from worship into work, to begin again the activity to which God has called us.

So before we go out to our work in the world, let's say these words together:

May this space be open, equal and accessible.
May our service be simple, humble and freely offered.
May our communion be sincere and available to all.
In the name of Christ, we pray it may be so.
Amen.

Silence

Closing responses:

As we perceive our need for wisdom,
Enlighten us, God.

As we look for you everywhere,
Reveal yourself, God.

As we attentively wait for you,
Give us patience, God.

As we reflect on you,
Open our hearts, God.

May we declare your truth in our lives.
**In the name of the Holy Three:
Creator, Son and Spirit.
Amen**

(Based on a prayer of St Benedict)

Notes:

1. Used with the permission of the Lay Community of St Benedict (www.laybenedictines.org).

2. I use the word 'kindom' to indicate a gender-neutral place and community gathered by God.

Living rough, living sheltered
A service of solidarity with rough sleepers

Urzula Glienecke

Welcome

Opening responses:

Holy Trinity, you welcome us into your family.
Remind us that we are all your children.

Loving God, you welcome us into the shelter of your care.
Remind us about our sisters and brothers who are without shelter.

Jesus Christ, you were a carpenter.
**Help us to work with you to build societies and systems
where there is a place for all.**

Holy Spirit, you inspire, challenge and connect us.
Bind us together into your network of one humanity.

Song

See Resources for some suggested songs and chants.

Word:

A scripture reading, a story from someone sleeping rough, a poem, a newspaper article on homelessness in your city …

See Resources for some suggested scripture readings and a collection of stories.

And/or a reflection on a piece of art or a photograph

Prayer of confession:

Caring God, Creator of all,
we confess the times when we have turned away.
Forgive us and melt our hearts.

We confess the times when we have walked on by.
Forgive us and melt our hearts.

We confess the times when we have judged someone
by their rough appearance;
when we have blamed someone
without knowing or understanding their life story;
when we have shunned someone
without knowing or understanding their pain;
when we have seen people not as people,
but as problems.

**Forgive us and turn our hearts into hearts of flesh
that beat with compassion and solidarity.**

Song or chant

Prayer of thanksgiving:

Jesus Christ, brother of all,
we thank you for showing us that we are all worthy of God's love.
You told stories about the poor, the outcast and the homeless
being invited to your wedding feast.
You touched those deemed untouchable;
you spoke to those no one spoke to;
you shared food with those excluded from the society.
And you asked these people what they wanted
and listened to them.

Holy Spirit, we thank you for all the times
you have moved our hearts to see, to reach out,
to listen, to walk beside people.

We thank you for all the people, organisations and movements
working to bring lasting change to our societies.
Loving God, we thank you for the privilege and joy
of being a part of your intention and work in the world.
Amen

A symbolic action:

Play some reflective music and invite folk to come up to the communion table to pick up a paper heart to take home with them: as a reminder of those living rough. Suggest that, the next time they're in town, they ask someone sleeping rough if they'd like a hot or cold drink, and get this for them, and one for themselves too, and then sit and chat with the person a while … and listen.

Affirmation of faith (after Matthew 25:35–40):

**We believe that when we share food with the hungry,
we share food with you.**

**We believe that when we share drink with the thirsty,
we share drink with you.**

**We believe that when we welcome the stranger,
we are blessed by your presence.**

**We believe that when we take care of the sick and visit the prisoner,
we become your community of love.**

**We believe that when we work on changing unjust systems,
we work to build your kingdom on earth.**

And Jesus will then answer us:

'Truly I tell you,
just as you did it to one of the least of these
who are members of my family,
you did it to me.'
Amen

Song

Blessing:

May God, in whose house there are many rooms, shelter us.
May Jesus, who had no place to lay his head, challenge us.
May the Spirit, She who is everywhere,
connect us all into one community that truly cares.
Amen

Resources

Suggested songs and chants

'Jesus Christ is waiting', John L Bell and Graham Maule, from *Heaven Shall Not Wait*, Wild Goose Publications

'Will you come and follow me?', John L Bell and Graham Maule, from *Love from Below*, Wild Goose Publications

'Enemy of apathy', John L Bell and Graham Maule, from *Enemy of Apathy*, Wild Goose Publications

'Beauty for brokenness', Graham Kendrick

'For everyone born, a place at the table', Shirley Erena Murray

'The kingdom of God is justice and peace', Taizé

'Ubi caritas', Taizé

Suggested scripture readings

Isaiah 25:4
Isaiah 58:7
Ezekiel 36:26
Matthew 8:20
Matthew 22 (The parable of the wedding feast)
Matthew 25:35

Luke 16:19–31 (The rich man and Lazarus)
John 1:48

Stories

These are stories of real lives and real people, only the names and slight details have been changed to protect privacy. Most of the people in the stories have passed away, as people on the streets often do unfortunately. A couple still live on – and I hope will do so as long as possible.

You could read these stories in a worship service, using different voices.

The man in the silk suit

Alex had been a manager of a large company, a high-flyer and successful. Then the financial crisis hit and the company went bankrupt. He couldn't continue paying for his large flat in the prestigious area of town. His girlfriend left him. One thing led to another, and now he's sitting on the street in the same shiny business district where he used to rush about. The only thing that remains from what once was is his silk jacket. 'At least it keeps me warm,' he says.

Queen Vera

Vera was born shortly after the war in the Soviet Union, no one knows exactly when. She was born 'without papers' and left at an orphanage. Her name then was Vitalij. She was adopted by a woman who lived in a communal flat. From early on, Vera knew she was different. When they poured a bath for her in the kitchen in the tin tub, every time a man entered, she hid. She didn't do that when women came in. When she was a teenager she was forced to go to the public baths – the men's ones, as her body was that of a man. Perpetrators sensed that she was different and wouldn't be protected. She was abused again and again.

Now she is an elderly queen who adores cats and has found her dignity. 'Cats are the love I lacked,' she says.

The woman with the cemetery flowers

Every day Eva stands on the bridge, just under the lamp, with a bunch of mismatched flowers of all colours and sizes imaginable. I know that every morning she makes her way out of the city to the big cemetery and collects the flowers left on the graves. I know, but buy them from her anyway. She says she would never beg. So, I buy the flowers, many the worse for wear, and she smiles.

The chemistry professor

Jacob used to be a chemistry professor at a university. He was proud of his job. But his country changed, the system changed, and left many unemployed. He was too old to find another job. Now he lives in an abandoned house, and gets the odd painting job. 'Well, that's almost chemistry too, you know,' he says.

The man with the dog called Rex

I see them sheltering from the wind and sleet in the doorway of a closed shop. The man and his shaggy, big shepherd dog. The dog wags his tail politely at me. 'His name is Rex,' the man says. 'It means king, you know.' And the dog is his king and companion. If there's food, Rex gets it first. They can't get into any of the hostels or shelters, not even in the foulest weather: no dogs allowed. 'I wouldn't go anywhere without Rex – no way!'

The woman with the loaded shopping cart

Lola pushes her loaded shopping cart through the city. It's covered in a worn plastic sheet against the rain. When the afternoon comes, she stops and unpacks her life onto the pavement. There's an old blanket and bags with this and that. And then the flowerpot comes out and the icon. She sets them lovingly against the wall. If she can, and isn't chased away, she chooses places where she can hear music coming from the bars. She loves music so.

The troublemaker

Mike lived on the street for 18 years. At the beginning, he ran away from home and stayed under the stars with his friends. Oh, they were troublemakers! All the pubs had a ban on them.

Mike tried to live 'a normal life' as a car mechanic, as a fuel station attendant. He married and had a child. But every time, the drink took him again. So his child, his boy, was taken away from him and then … he completely lost it. He drank and drank and drank. He was beaten and drenched with water in the freezing wintertime; chased from place to place. But he stayed in the town where he was born, no matter what they did to him. Until one morning he was found dead. Dead on the street of the town where he was born.

What was Mike's pain? Why did he run away from home at the start? What did he need to drown in drink? Nobody will know now.

The girl who draws

Ila holds a piece of chalk in her trembling fingers. Her inflamed joints burn in the cold of the autumn evening. The chalk, she found just outside the school. She goes looking for some and then draws abstract shapes on the wall, and then steps back to look at them. And then she draws some more. The shapes cascade down like seaweed, like ice flowers on a windowpane. When the rain comes the chalk runs down the wall and blends. And she watches it go. Her grandmother tried to smother her in her sleep. With a pillow, white as chalk. So she ran away. And Ila lets the chalk get washed away in the rain.

Remember me
Resources for the United Nations International Day for the Eradication of Poverty (17th October)

John Harvey, Ian M Fraser and Kathy Galloway

Reflection: the Poverty Stone

'I wept buckets when I heard my son telling his pals that he'd had a big plate of mince and tatties for his dinner, when I knew that all I had been able to give him was a bowl of porridge.'

'I bear witness to a single parent with a six-year-old son, homeless due to break-ins to her flat. She's been trying to get a private let for six months, but because she is on benefits she's been excluded, and made to feel in a different social class and segregated from those who have money.'

'I just wish I could go into a shop once, and buy a leg of lamb.'[1]

Facts and figures about poverty are well known. But the voices of those who live in poverty are seldom heard – and rarely listened to.

Every year, on October 17th, there's a gathering in Glasgow's George Square, round the Poverty Stone, to mark the United Nations International Day for the Eradication of Poverty. Here's where the real experts in poverty – those who actually live in it – tell their stories, sing their songs, share their frustration and their anger, and demand the right to be heard by the people in power. It's an annual event, sponsored by Glasgow's Poverty Truth Community – with their motto *'Nothing about us, without us, is for us'* – and ATD Fourth World. It's been happening every year since 1992.

This is no greetin' meetin' of people feeling sorry for themselves. ATD Fourth World (All Together in Dignity to Overcome Poverty), for instance, grew out of the experience of a Catholic Priest, Joseph Wresinski, who had lived for years with homeless families in an emergency housing camp in France. There, he came to realise that the appalling nature of their conditions was basically a denial of their human rights. He founded ATD in 1957; and in 1987 ATD laid the first Poverty Stone in Paris, bearing Wresinski's words: 'Wherever men and women are condemned to live in poverty, human rights are violated. To come together to ensure that these rights are respected is our solemn duty.' Today, ATD has over 375 volunteers in 35 countries, supporting families making spaces to express themselves, creating dialogue, reflecting and cooperating with others to work their way into places of power, where poverty can be challenged, and changed.

Glasgow's Poverty Stone is one of over 50 replicas of the original stone, in many countries worldwide. A small group of volunteers from Glasgow Braendam Link (GBL), a local charity working in partnership with people living in poverty, pestered Glasgow City Council for years. The Council wanted it to be in a Peace Garden by the Cathedral. GBL insisted it had to be in the very heart of the city. In 1999 the Council gave in, and the Poverty Stone was laid on October 17th of that year.

The Poverty Truth Commission (PTC) movement is another opportunity for the voices of people living in poverty to be heard – and not only to be heard, but to be seriously listened to by the people in power. It started in Glasgow twelve years ago, and has spread to a number of other cities across the UK. The PTC brings together folk from opposite sides of the poverty gap, not to shout at each other, but to struggle together to find ways of tackling vital issues – knife crime, media bias, low wages, discrimination, racial and sexual prejudice, poor housing and education – seeking together to understand, and change, things for the better.

Like many other groups across the UK, including APLE (APLE Collective: Addressing Poverty with Lived Experience), we will be meeting again this year, on 17th October. The buzz will be powerful, the stories telling, the hope and the determination so strong. Please join us if you can – at midday, in George Square in Glasgow, round the Poverty Stone. And if you can't join us, please be with us in spirit and solidarity on that day and take a moment to remember people living in poverty, here in the UK and throughout the world.

John Harvey

Prayer

Lord God, you humble me before the poor.
The more I have the more I want to cling to.
Jesus Christ did not grasp at divine equality but laid aside his glory,
stripping himself of privilege and security
to live life with the conditions we live under.

He was a vulnerable child, unprotected from Herod's wrath, a refugee;
he was found alongside the lowest, the least, the lost,
he gave all, even life itself.
Yet I hesitate to part with some of my abundance.

Lord God, you humble me before the poor
who when they have a little to eat, share it,
who will fight to secure others' good,
who, having nothing, yet seem to possess all things.
What must I do to be saved?
If we all become poor, there would not even be a portion for each.
I cringe away from the sacrifice Jesus asked of the rich young man.
But I also believe I am not called to part with my possessions as he was.
Or am I? Search my heart; you know my innermost thoughts.
Teach me so to handle the possessions you have entrusted to me
that whatsoever is asked of me,
they will be treated as yours, not as my own.
Teach me grace to give whatever you require of me,
and grace to refuse whatever mistaken pressures guilt would exact from me.
Teach me to fight unjust systems which rob people
of their share of God's provision.

Teach me to be alert to rationalisations and evasions in my own life
and in Church and in public life.

May I respond to Mary's vision – of the poor lifted high.
All this I ask in Jesus Christ's name and for his sake.
Amen [2]

Ian M Fraser

Remember me

Do you remember me?

Though I am nameless to you
and have no statue or square in my honour,
you will look down and I will be there,
under your feet,
close to the earth where I lived and died.
I could not rise where you might look up to me on a plinth or plate;
too many burdens pinned me down.
Narrow sunless streets and overcrowded closes hemmed me in;
I breathed damp and foetid air from running walls
and cholera, typhoid, tuberculosis, asthma laid me low.
Polio, rickets and poor food shortened my stature and my days,
and heroin and AIDS cut me down.

Remember me, do you?

I turned the wheels that made the engine-room roar.
I dug your roads and built your ships,
I carted your coal and drove your trains,
I forged your iron and unloaded your docks,
I stoked your boilers and fed your production lines,
I cleaned your offices and swept your streets,
I sewed your clothes and emptied your bins,
I made your weapons and fought your wars,
I fried your food and guarded your factories,
until you had no more use for me
and I became an economic liability.
I came from many places to do it:
from the Highland glens and island shores,
from the slave-mines of Ayrshire and the valleys of Lanark,
from Ireland, Poland, Russia, Italy,
from India, Pakistan, Uganda, China,
from Chile, Vietnam, Iraq and Kosovo;
well that you remember me on the ground beneath your feet.
The city was built on my labour.

You remember me?

Remember the miracles I worked, on low pay, or no pay,
on strike pay or benefit.
Remember the washing I did,
walls, stairs, clothes, weans;
remember the lullabies I sang them when they couldn't sleep,
and the nights I sat up with a sick neighbour.
Remember the wakes when they died.
Remember the allotments I dug
and the jerseys I knitted
and the houses I painted;
remember the matches, the beautiful game.
Remember the singing, remember the dances;
remember the patter, and the drinking, and the laughter,
remember the courting and the weddings and the babies.
Remember the young ones who made it to college,
and the others who didn't, remember them too.
Remember the unions and the co-ops and the tenants' groups,
remember the marches to the Green and the Square.
Remember the suffragettes and the rent strikes, and the poll tax –
remember we tried and we fought and we cared.
Remember that I kept on getting up every morning,
remember my prayers and remember my tears.
Remember that I lived and my life had a value,
remember that I loved and hungered for more:
for the chance to reach out and look up and see further,
for a life free of want and exhaustion and fear;
for the right to be treated with justice and dignity,
for the right to be human,
for the right to a name.
It's not much to ask, but it's harder to come by,
and it's hardest of all to be seen when you're poor.
So when you walk by, just stop for a moment
and see me, and wonder, and maybe ask 'why?'
And you remember me.[3]

Kathy Galloway

Written for the laying of a stone in George Square, Glasgow, to commemorate all those who have been victims of poverty.

Information, stories, resources, ideas for action

APLE Collective: Addressing Poverty with Lived Experience: www.aplecollective.com

ATD Fourth World:
https://atd-uk.org

Christian Aid: www.christianaid.org.uk

Church Action on Poverty: www.church-poverty.org.uk

Glasgow Braendam Link (GBL)/The Lilias Graham Trust:
http://thelgt.org.uk/our-history

Poverty Truth Community/Faith in Community Scotland:
www.faithincommunity.scot/poverty-truth-community

Sources and acknowledgements:

1. Quotes from people who were attending an October 17th event in George Square, Glasgow, from an unpublished paper – these were all people living in poverty.

2. Adapted from *Strange Fire: Life Stories and Prayers,* by Ian M Fraser, Wild Goose Publications, 1994

3. From *The Dream of Learning Our True Name*, Kathy Galloway, Wild Goose Publications, 2004

Stones and bread, mourning and joy
Resources for Trans Day of Remembrance (20th November)

Alex Clare-Young

Invocation:

We come asking for mercy.
Meet us, merciful God.

We come in need of clarity.
Help us, teaching God.

We come angry at injustice.
Hear us, reconciling God.

We come with our hands full of stones.
Feed us, caring God.

Reading:
Matthew 7:1–10 (NIV)[1]

'Do not judge, or you too will be judged. For in the same way you judge others, you will be judged, and with the measure you use, it will be measured to you.

'Why do you look at the speck of sawdust in your brother's eye and pay no attention to the plank in your own eye? How can you say to your brother, "Let me take the speck out of your eye," when all the time there is a plank in your own eye? You hypocrite, first take the plank out of your own eye, and then you will see clearly to remove the speck from your brother's eye.

'Do not give dogs what is sacred; do not throw your pearls to pigs. If you do, they may trample them under their feet, and turn and tear you to pieces.

'Ask and it will be given to you; seek and you will find; knock and the door will be opened to you. For everyone who asks receives; the one who seeks finds; and to the one who knocks, the door will be opened.

'Which of you, if your son asks for bread, will give him a stone? Or if he asks for a fish, will give him a snake?' …

Reflection:

It seems to be becoming harder, not easier, to be a trans person. Around the world, political, societal and religious realities mean that trans lives are more often judged than respected, more often trampled under feet than treasured. And yet, trans people are increasingly sharing narratives of euphoria rather than dysphoria; joy rather than mourning; resilience rather than resignation. We are asking for bread, rather than stones. This isn't an easy shift though. Nor is it a sign that our lives aren't difficult, our dysphoria isn't real. Rather, trans people are increasingly trying to rewrite our own stories. We are knocking on your door; will you answer? We are seeking help; will we find it?

'Hang on,' you might protest, 'we have been through a pandemic and Brexit, and are experiencing increasing poverty and division. Don't we have enough to deal with?' And there are, indeed, countless tugs on our resources of time, energy and money. Nevertheless, our reading today calls us to be active, rather than passive. One of the hardest questions to answer is the question of why God allows injustice to continue. This reading is clear, though, that we have a role, a responsibility, in creating a just world. We have to keep knocking until those in power give all people bread, not stones. We must keep opening doors, until those who close them give up. Trans people are asking for bread, and we are still being given stones.

In the UK, where I live, 76% of non-binary people, like me, said that they avoid expressing their gender identity out in public for fear of negative reactions and/or abuse and a third had experienced hate crimes. And this is before we even consider the trans lives lost to violence and hatred worldwide, which also disproportionately affects women, feminine people, Black and Brown people, young people and poor people. In other words, the trans lives lost are indicative of the patterns of intersectional oppression against which we must take a stand. We must say their names. And we must feel the heartbreak of those who love the people whose names are still unknown.

The story of JJ and Jasmine is a heart-rending example of what we have lost. Jeffrey 'JJ' Bright, a 16-year-old trans boy, and his sister Jasmine Cannady, a 22-year-old non-binary person, were killed in Pennsylvania in their own home. Jeffrey was known for his laugh and his jokes. Jasmine was described as 'a sweet, shy and artistic soul' as well as a deeply caring friend. Their favourite quote was 'Don't let anyone bring you down. Don't let people tell you that you can't do anything in life. You mean something.'[2]

And so, with JJ and Jasmine in mind, I ask you again: We are knocking on your door; will you answer? We are seeking help; will we find it?

Act of remembrance:

The Act of Remembrance is central to a Trans Day of Remembrance service. Some facilitators read out the names of those lost in the past year. Others provide a list of names, which participants may read during a time of silence or music. I would encourage facilitators to consider researching and sharing the stories of one or more trans people lost during the past year. This can help us to remember the value, joy and struggles of their lives, rather than reducing those we mourn for to the brutal, unchosen realities of their deaths. There is a list of links that may help you to facilitate this time of remembrance at the end of this resource.

If you are using the following letting go activity, give each participant a stone, and then invite participants to decorate their stones with paint, paint-pens, markers or chalk, or to hold on to their stones during this time of remembrance. If you are following this resource alone, or as part of a digital gathering, you may wish to decorate a stone, or a piece of clay, or a piece of paper or other material shaped into a stone or cairn, as a version of the activity below and to remind you of those who have died, and of our commitment to change.

Letting go activity:

You each have a decorated stone. In our reading and reflection, we considered the harsh reality of asking for bread, and being given stones. And so, perhaps these stones might represent the painful realities of the lives that we have lost, and the oppression, discrimination, marginalisation and abuse that trans people experience.

Stones can also, however, be used to build, to celebrate, to remember and to inspire change. A cairn is a pile or stack of stones; the word comes from the Gaelic word *càrn*. Cairns are traditionally built for many reasons, one of which is remembrance.

Today, let's put down our stones, our pain, our complicity and our silence. Let's build a cairn to inspire actions of transformation, of speaking out, of justice.

Whilst music plays, or in silence, invite participants to add their stones to a pile of stones at the front or centre of the gathering.

Intercessions:

Let us pray:

Jesus teaches: 'Do not judge, or you too will be judged.'
We pray for those who are struggling to let go of norms, judgements and stereotypes.
Creator God, transformational Spirit, we pray for change.

Jesus explains: 'First take the plank out of your own eye, and then you will see clearly.'
We pray for ourselves, that we might grow in understanding.
Creator God, transformational Spirit, we pray for change.

Jesus suggests: 'Ask and it will be given to you.'
We pray for those asking for help.
Creator God, transformational Spirit, we pray for change.

Jesus urges: 'Seek and you will find.'
We pray for those seeking an increase in hope, joy and fullness of life.
Creator God, transformational Spirit, we pray for change.

Jesus assures: 'Knock and the door will be opened to you.'
We pray for those working hard to open doors.
Creator God, transformational Spirit, we pray for change.

Jesus asks: 'Which of you, if your child asks for bread, will give them a stone?'
We pray for those putting down their stones and asking for bread.
Creator God, transformational Spirit, we pray for change.
Amen.

Going out:

As you leave this place, take a stone to remind you of the cairn we have built together, and of the work that we still need to do if we are to offer bread and life.

Remember those we have lost.
Remember those we care for.
Remember to let God,
Creator, Redeemer and Sustainer,
weave the possibility of transformation through your days.
We will remember.
Amen.

Recommended resources

For more information about the statistics included in this reflection, visit:

https://www.gov.uk/government/publications/national-lgbt-survey-summary-report/national-lgbt-survey-summary-report

For more resources about Trans Day of Remembrance (TDoR), including this year's names and the stories of those who have died, visit:

https://transrespect.org/en/trans-murder-monitoring

For a different resource for TDoR, visit:

https://www.ionabooks.com/product/transgender-day-of-remembrance-pdf-download

To hear the stories of two trans people, and to learn more about our identities, consider reading:

https://www.ionabooks.com/product/dazzling-darkness-new-revised-edition

https://www.ionabooks.com/product/transgender-christian-human

To join, or find out more about, the Iona Community's LGBTQ+ Common Concern Network, or for support around the identities and topics considered in this resource, e-mail Alex Clare-Young at: ccnlgbtq@iona.org.uk

Notes:

1. Holy Bible, New International Version® Anglicised, NIV® Copyright © 1979, 1984, 2011 by Biblica, Inc.® Used by permission. All rights reserved worldwide.

2. www.hrc.org/news/hrc-mourns-jeffrey-jj-bright-trans-teen-killed-in-pennsylvania

That further shore
A simple liturgy for remembering someone who has died

Simon Taylor

Introduction:

These words, prayers and poems help us to remember the person who was with us on this shore but departs now to that further shore. We remember how they blessed us, we express our grief and we seek God's comfort.

Through these reflections, we begin to let go of our loved one or friend, releasing them into the eternal love of God, and seeking the support of God and one another as we journey on together here.

We pause this day to remember the life of *(name)*.

We seek God's help and strength …

Verses from the Bible:

The eternal God is our refuge, and underneath are the everlasting arms.
Deuteronomy 33:27 (NIV)

God is our refuge and strength, a very present help in trouble.
Psalm 46:1 (NRSV)

Jesus said, 'Do not let your hearts be troubled. Believe in God, believe also in me. In my Father's house there are many dwelling places. If it were not so, would I have told you that I go to prepare a place for you? And if I go and prepare a place for you, I will come again and will take you to myself, so that where I am, there you may be also.'
John 14:1–3 (NRSV)

We take a moment of quiet as we recall our *loved one/friend* …

Prayer:

God of love,
we voice our sorrow at this parting
and seek your comfort in the pain of our loss.
We draw close to you in our need,

trusting in the depth of your compassion
revealed in Jesus, our hope.

Lord, our hearts are heavy with grief;
we struggle to accept what has happened.
We come to you in need of your strength and support;
walk with us in our sorrow and give us your comfort.

Help us to give thanks for the life of *(name)*;
as we reflect upon our memories of *her/him*,
may we find joy in them
and celebrate how *her/his* life blessed ours.

Give us hope in the light of your love,
for Jesus died and lives again,
bringing us the gift of eternal peace
in the arms of our ever-living God.
Amen

Remembering how they blessed us:

We give thanks …

Remember moments shared with our friend/loved one on this shore …

Think of what made them special …

Think of time spent together …

Think about what we valued about them …

Think about how they made us smile or gave us encouragement …

Think about how their life blessed ours …

Spend a few moments giving thanks to God for *her/his* life …

Loving God,
we thank you for the gift of human love and friendship.
We celebrate all the ways that *(name)* blessed our lives
and give you thanks for *her/his* life.

For all that *she/he* meant to us,
for all that *she/he* shared with us,
for all that *she/he* gave to us,
we say thank you.

We give you thanks:

for everything that made them special to us,
for every way *her/his* life touched ours,
for everything *her/his* life inspired or encouraged,
for each of our memories and recollections of *her/him*.

We thank you for the love that surrounded *her/him*,
and for all those who cared for *her/him*,
through all *her/his* days.
Amen

Expressing our grief and seeking God's comfort:

We pray for all who mourn …

Think of those who mourn for *(name)*.
Ask God to be with them,
to hold them and comfort them.

Think of your own sadness at the death of *(name)*.
Ask God to be with you,
to hold you and comfort you.

God of comfort,
you are our help in every time of trouble.
Hold us in this present moment,
for we believe you know our grief
and you share our sense of loss.

Comfort all who mourn for *(name)*;
comfort me in my pain at this parting.

Enfold us in your peace,
surround us with your love,
hold us in your care,
so that in our sorrow
we will know the nearness of your strength …

Comforting God,
in Jesus you saw the grief of those who mourned:
watch now with us in our sorrow
and enfold us with your love.

Comforting God,
in Jesus you shed tears as you felt the loss of a friend:
be with us now as our tears flow
and comfort us with your presence.

Comforting God,
in Jesus you journeyed into the darkness of death:
be with our friend
as *she/he* departs toward another shore.

Comforting God,
in Jesus you rose again to new life,
overcoming the hold of death.

Bring our *friend/loved one* to that new dawn
where all is light and peace.
Amen

We say goodbye …

Spend a few moments giving *(name)* into the hands of God, who knows *her/him* by name and whose care is perfect and eternal …

Bible reading and reflection:

> *As for me ... the time of my departure has come. I have fought the good fight, I have finished the race, I have kept the faith. From now on there is reserved for me the crown of righteousness, which the Lord, the righteous judge, will give me on that day, and not only to me but also to all who have longed for his appearing.*
>
> 2 Timothy 4:6–8 (NRSV)

The phrase the Apostle Paul uses for death, 'the time of departure', was used to describe a ship setting sail and voyaging to another shore. As we acknowledge the departure of our *loved one/friend* from this life, we let *her/him* go to journey with God as *her/his* guide to that further shore where there is no anxiety, no pain and no more sorrow.

Prayer:

Loving God,
as *(name)* now journeys to another shore,
to that place where all is rest and peace,
keep *her/him* ever in your loving care.

Reassure us in knowing
that you journey with us in life and through death.
And now that the tide has turned,
and it is time to let *(name)* go,
help us to give *her/him* into your care;
bring *her/him* safely to that further shore
into your welcoming embrace and eternal light.

A time of quiet

We seek strength to carry on.

As *(name)* sets sail,
be near to we who are left:
comfort us as we wave our farewell from this shore,

encourage us with the love you give
and bring us joy through the memories we hold.

May we find hope in knowing that, one day,
we too will walk on that further shore,
for you have shown us that the grave is not the end
and your love holds us through all things.

Walk with us as we learn to live with our loss.
Enable us to console and support one another;
may your compassion surround us,
may your strength sustain us,
that in the days to come
we may see not only our sorrow
but the dawning of hope
in the Christ who died yet lives again.

Poem:

Some suggestions for a poem to finish on.

I am standing upon the seashore

I am standing upon the seashore.
A ship at my side spreads her white
sails to the morning breeze and starts for the blue ocean.

She is an object of beauty and strength,
and I stand and watch her until at length
she hangs like a speck of white cloud
just where the sea and sky come
to mingle with each other.

Then, someone at my side says:
'There, she is gone!'

'Gone where?'

Gone from my sight. That is all.
She is just as large in mast and hull

and spar as she was when she left my side
and she is just as able to bear her
load of living freight to her destined port.
Her diminished size is in me, not in her.

And just at the moment when someone
at my side says, 'There, she is gone!'
There are other eyes watching her coming,
and other voices ready to take up the glad shout:
'Here she comes!'
And that is dying.

Attributed to Rev Luther F Beecher (1813–1903), Henry Van Dyke (1852–1933), and sometimes Victor Hugo

Winter storms

Life spreads out before me,
an unpredictable expanse of steely water.
The shore is beyond the reach of my mind.
My little boat tosses and flips in the water –
too small to be significant;
too loved to be turned away.

My Lord to whom the waves answer,
remind me that your presence calms the storm.

When the storm grows strong around me,
when the water comes lashing in,
remind me that I am never alone.
Spread your arms wide to save me.
Welcome home your lost child.

My Lord to whom the winds answer,
remind me that your presence calms the storm.

Lord, Creator of all,
show me the horizon beyond the waves,
the land where I will take my rest.

Guide me through the mist,
through the uncharted waters.

My Lord to whom the tides answer,
lead me to the shore where I will walk with you.

Kira Taylor

Crossing the bar

Sunset and evening star,
　And one clear call for me!
And may there be no moaning of the bar,
　When I put out to sea,

But such a tide as moving seems asleep,
　Too full for sound and foam,
When that which drew from out the boundless deep
　Turns again home.

Twilight and evening bell,
　And after that the dark!
And may there be no sadness of farewell,
　When I embark;

For tho' from out our bourne of Time and Place
　The flood may bear me far,
I hope to see my Pilot face to face
　When I have crost the bar.

Alfred Lord Tennyson (1809–1892)

Blessing:

We journey on in God's strength:

God the Father keep you in his care,
God the Son fill your life with love and hope,
God the Spirit comfort you and give you peace.
Amen

Sources and acknowledgements

Passages from NRSV copyright 1989, Division of Christian Education of the National Council of the Churches of Christ in the United States of America. Used by permission. All rights reserved.

Scripture quotations taken from The Holy Bible, New International Version® NIV®Copyright © 1973 1978 1984 2011 by Biblica, Inc. TM Used by permission. All rights reserved worldwide.

Rest beside quiet waters
A reflection for caregivers who may feel wearied

Elaine Gisbourne

In 2015 I wrote 'Called to be an innkeeper', a reflection on the parable of the Good Samaritan, for all those who care for others.[1]

Now, in response to the Covid-19 pandemic, I have revisited that piece and reflected on Psalm 23, in order to hear God's healing voice for all caregivers who may feel wearied by the task.

My sick ones came to you,
and you did not turn away.
You stayed with them when those they love
could not hold their hands and tend them.

You faced your own fears,
as you drew close to theirs;
and walked with so many
through the valley of their death,
for some, to your own.

I grieve for each of my loved ones now silent.
I hold them, for none are lost to me.

Beloved caregiver,
I draw close to tend to you.
My steadfast heart is wide open;
I hear your whispered sorrow,
embrace the storm of your rage,
calm your anxious thoughts.
Trust in me and in my promises:
I will never leave you.

I sit beside you,
that you may lean on me;
pour on you my healing love
to revive your parched soul;
spread before you good things
to nourish and restore.

Find peace in the beauty of the world,
joy in the friendship of those you love
and know that my delight is in you,
whom I love.

Note:

1. 'Called to be an innkeeper: A reflection on Luke 10:25–37, the Good Samaritan', Elaine Gisbourne, Wild Goose Publications:

www.ionabooks.com/product/called-to-be-an-innkeeper-pdf-download

Shining the light of Christ into a world of conflict
A liturgy and resources for Remembrance Sunday

Nancy Cocks

Introduction:

In the United Kingdom, Remembrance Sunday is marked on the Sunday closest to November 11, known as 'Armistice Day' or 'Remembrance Day', the day hostilities in World War One ended in 1918. Other countries offer remembrance on different days according to their own histories in conflict. These resources have the UK tradition in mind, but provide ideas or items which may be adapted for worship on this theme in other locations. However, lectionary references for other Sundays will vary.

To lead into the Act of Remembrance, you need seven candles to light and a hammer with a piece of wood solid enough to receive seven blows. Instead of using a hammer, you can ring a resonant bell after each of the biddings. Following the Act of Remembrance, the liturgy includes lighting the Christ Candle.

Song suggestions are included in the Appendix section. There is an optional symbolic action for children included in the Appendix too.

Before the service, you may wish to remind people to be sure their mobile phones have been silenced.

Opening responses:

From Micah 4:2–4

Leader: Come, let us go up to the mountain of the Lord,
People: **that God may teach us God's ways
and we may walk in God's paths.**

Leader: Our God shall arbitrate for many peoples;
between strong nations far away,
People: **and they shall beat their swords into ploughshares,
and their spears into pruning-hooks.**

Leader: Nation shall not lift up sword against nation,
People: **neither shall they learn war any more.**

Leader: They shall all sit under their own vines and fruit trees;
People: **and no one shall make them afraid.**

Song

Opening prayers:

Leader: We gather at this solemn time, O God,
aware of the costliness of human history.
In the face of hostility between nations and neighbours,
you have come to us in Jesus Christ,
offering us the gift of peace, calling us to serve as peacemakers.
In this time of worship,
renew in us the hope that you will
turn our swords into ploughshares,
and by the power of the Holy Spirit,
lead the world you love away from the study of war
to the promise of peace with justice for all your peoples.

Unison:

**God of mercy,
we confess that the world around us is in a mess.
Countries turn disputes over territory into acts of terror.
Old enemies stir up conflict within their tribes and nations.
The threat of violence keeps us all on edge.
Forgive us for not learning from past conflicts
what will lead to peace with justice;
forgive us when we harbour a desire to settle our own old scores
and keep conflict alive.**

Sung response: 'Kyrie eleison, Christe eleison, Kyrie eleison'

Or 'Dona nobis pacem'

Or substitute a similar spoken response.

God's word of mercy:

Option one, from John 14:27

Leader: Jesus said, 'Peace I leave with you; my peace I give unto you. Not as the world gives do I give to you. The peace of our Lord Jesus Christ be with you.'

People: **And also with you.**

Option two, from Micah 6:8

Leader: The prophet Micah declared that God requires of us three things: to do justice, to love kindness, and to walk humbly with our God.

To all who turn away from hostility and seek reconciliation with God and neighbour in kindness and humility, God offers forgiveness and peace.

The peace of our Lord Jesus Christ be with you all.

People: **And also with you.**

Song

A call to remembrance:

Leader: Remembrance pulses at the centre of Christian faith, drawing on its roots within Jewish tradition and its practice in every human community across generations and cultures. The Scriptures carry memories of events foundational to our trust in God, as well as wisdom from earlier generations of the faithful, which continue to shape our liturgies through remembrance. The symbols we recognise and the creeds we recite carry meaning rooted in remembrance. Holy Communion calls us to remember Jesus Christ, his grace and his mercy. Remembrance beats at the heart of Christian worship, connecting each generation with the communion of saints through the power of the Holy Spirit. We too will be remembered, even after we are gone.

The connection we feel with those who have gone before us enlivens our acts of remembrance, evoking our gratitude for the lasting benefits of their service. Their best examples of courage, compassion, justice and generosity continue to inspire us. Yet there are also past examples of which we are not proud, things we hope we will never repeat, things we must learn from. For us, George Santayana's famous quotation remains a touchstone: *'Those who cannot remember the past are condemned to repeat it.'*[1]

We mark Remembrance Sunday in the hope that we will remember the costliness of war, not only the wars of the twentieth century which engulfed so much of the world, but also the smaller yet deadly conflicts of this century. For it surely seems there are lessons as yet unlearned while violent conflicts take repeated tolls on human communities and the very fabric of God's creation.

In this service, we remember lessons from past and current conflicts, not to celebrate victories – which have often proven short-lived – but rather to honour lives lost,to pray for those who still pay the costs of conflict, and to seek God's wisdom in following paths of justice and cooperation which can lead to peace for all the creatures and communities of God's abiding love.

Readings from Scripture:

See Appendix for readings in the Revised Common Lectionary.

Reflection on the Word and Wisdom of God:

Suggestions:

- *If there are children present for the service, you could invite them to share in a symbolic action while they listen to reflections more suited to adult listeners. See the Appendix for the suggestion called 'Hands of remembrance'. If you choose to do this action, use it before offering a reflection more suited to adult congregants.*

- *Prepare a meditation or sermon on one or more of the Scripture texts for the day.*

- *Offer a reading from a novel that explores the costliness of conflict. See A*

Very Long Engagement, by Sébastien Japrisot; *Birdsong*, by Sebastian Faulks; *Obasan*, by Joy Kogawa; *Suite Française*, by Irène Némirovsky; *The Splendid and the Vile*, by Erik Larson …

- *Have different voices read poetry from different authors and/or eras. An Internet search for 'war poetry' will offer many selections, including traditional Remembrance Day poems like John McCrae's 'In Flanders Fields' (1915) or Lawrence Binyon's 'For the fallen' (1914).*

Song

The act of remembrance:

This section leads into a two-minute silence. It begins with lighting seven candles which are arranged centrally; followed by a hammer striking wood seven times. Or, instead of using a hammer sound, you can choose to ring a resonant bell after those biddings. (The bell became a symbol of The Law of the Innocents, developed and promulgated in 697 by Adomnán mac Rónáin, 9th Abbot of Iona, which protected children, women and priests in times of conflict.) If you use a bell, test out its resonance in advance of the service to be sure the sound carries. If you use a hammer on wood, test it out in advance to make sure the wood is resting on a secure base which is thick enough so that the hammer sound resonates.

Allow a 5-10 second pause between each of the bidding statements.

Light from lives we remember:

Leader: We light this candle in grateful, compassionate remembrance of those who gave their lives in conflict with bravery and with honour, in the service of their nation, to defeat the power of tyranny, defend justice and protect the vulnerable.

People: **We will remember.**

A candle is lit.

Leader: We light this candle in grateful, compassionate remembrance of those wounded in conflict, who came home bearing scars in body, mind and soul, and continue to bear the cost of their service for a lifetime.

People: **We will remember.**

A candle is lit.

Leader: We light this candle in grateful, compassionate remembrance of those who served in conflict zones whilst caring for the injured, praying with them, feeding them, reporting the truth from the front, facing danger themselves and witnessing horrors day by day.

People: **We will remember.**

A candle is lit.

Leader: We light this candle in grateful, compassionate remembrance of those who have lost loved ones through war – spouses, parents, children, lovers, friends and neighbours – who had to carry on with broken hearts and lives reshaped forever.

People: **We will remember.**

A candle is lit.

Leader: We light this candle in grateful, compassionate remembrance of those civilians who lost their lives or their livelihoods, their homes and communities through conflict fought on their streets, in their fields, and over their heads.

People: **We will remember.**

A candle is lit.

Leader: We light this candle in grateful, compassionate remembrance of the land, sea and sky ripped apart in battle, scarred by weaponry, and of all the creatures, wild or tame, who became victims of human hubris.

People: **We will remember.**

A candle is lit.

Leader: We light this candle in grateful, compassionate remembrance of every act of courage and compassion in the contexts of war, taken by soldier or citizen, politician or peacemaker, trusting that goodness could prevail.

People: **We will remember.**

A candle is lit.

Hard lessons from wartime:

Leader: We remember and lament the lies told to justify war and fuel hatred of 'enemies', knowing with regret that *'in war, truth is the first casualty'.*[2]

People: **God, have mercy.**

Strike the hammer or sound the bell.

Leader: We remember and lament the arrogance that has driven the desire to acquire more land, resources and power, igniting battles to claim them.

People: **God, have mercy.**

Strike the hammer or sound the bell.

Leader: We remember and lament the profiteering on weaponry and the diabolical schemes which created poisons and plans to annihilate others.

People: **God, have mercy.**

Strike the hammer or sound the bell.

Leader: We remember and lament the costs of wartime spending, diverting essential economic and human resources from tending to the common good and the needs of the most vulnerable.

Shining the light of Christ into a world of conflict 203

People: **God, have mercy.**

Strike the hammer or sound the bell.

Leader: We remember and lament the war crimes which exerted cruelty on opponents and broke international agreements on the conduct of combat and the defence of human rights.

People: **God, have mercy.**

Strike the hammer or sound the bell.

Leader: We remember and lament the manipulation at work when peace treaties were negotiated, exerting the agendas of the strongest nations over the interests of justice and renewal for all God's people.

People: **God, have mercy.**

Strike the hammer or sound the bell.

Leader: We remember and lament the resentments that lingered after wars ended, which so often simmered and then ignited into renewed conflict.

People: **God, have mercy.**

Strike the hammer or sound the bell.

Leader: Please stand, if you are able, as we hold two minutes of reverent silence to remember these lives and these lessons.

Some traditions allow for the use of 'The last post' and 'Reveille' played on the trumpet to bracket the two minutes of silence.

Two minutes of silence

Some traditions allow for the singing of the Royal Anthem (or a national anthem) during worship. If this is your tradition, have the musician/s begin the anthem at the end of the two minutes of silence.

Shining the Light of Christ into a world of conflict:

Leader: In the Word was life, and the life was the light of all people. The light shines in the darkness, and the darkness did not overcome it. (John 1:4–5)

Light the Christ Candle.

Song or solo

If the service includes an Offering, place it here.

If you invited children to prepare 'hands of remembrance', collect them with the offering. Or if no offering is taken up, arrange to collect the paper hands, or have the children bring them forward before the prayers for the world.

Prayers for the world:

God of all the ages past, hope of years to come,
we gather to remember in this time of forgetting,
grateful that you hold each one of us in your memory and your mystery,
now and for all the time to come.
God, in your mercy,
Hear our prayers.

Today we remember all those who died,
serving the purposes of justice and freedom from tyranny,
in the wars of the last century,
in conflicts of our own generation,
and in peacekeeping and relief efforts around the world.

Keep ten seconds of silence.

We remember their courage with gratitude,
and we remember their families who still ache for lives surrendered
at great cost.
God, in your mercy,
Hear our prayers.

Today we remember the victims of conflict,
hiding in forgotten corners of the world or making headlines in our news,
fearing death and destruction with each haunting sound,
longing for safety and peace.
We remember regions and nations engulfed in brutal conflict these days,
praying for …

Here name conflict zones in the current news.

Keep ten seconds of silence.

God, in your mercy,
Hear our prayers.

We remember peacekeepers and peacemakers,
serving the cause of peace with justice in many different ways.
We remember all who serve on peacekeeping missions,
monitoring tense situations
and intervening to prevent violence and intimidation.
We remember diplomats and aid workers,
peacemaking teams, ecumenical accompaniers and observer groups,
offering their skills to reduce tensions and protect vulnerable communities.
And we remember those who protest war and the use of nuclear arms,
raising voices and risking imprisonment to keep the world safe.

Keep ten seconds of silence.

God, in your mercy,
Hear our prayers.

We remember victims of violence in our own country,
still fearful and uncertain of the future.
Help us remember to speak out for their protection and recovery.
We remember all those around us who carry on
under the burden of sad and hard memories;
those weighed down by grief, disappointment, by anger, pain and loss;
and those whose service for others leaves them with trauma
they cannot forget.

Keep ten seconds of silence.

Help us remember to offer understanding hearts, listening ears
and the kinds of support they need most.
God, in your mercy,
Hear our prayers.

We also remember those who struggle to remember day by day;
those who face the fear of forgetting those who matter most to them
and the fear of being forgotten.

If you have had the children make hands of remembrance, add this:

O God, we also ask you to remember the names of those we have written on these hands of remembrance.

If there are a few names or phrases submitted, read them out.

O God, write all these names on the palms of your hands and remember them always.

Keep ten seconds of silence.

Help us remember to reach out in comfort and support
so that no one is forgotten.
God, in your mercy,
Hear our prayers.

God of all the ages past, hope of years to come,
help us remember you day by day.
Keep us faithful to the truth as your Spirit reveals it to us in prayerful, honest reflection.
Give us courage to make friends of enemies
and offer generosity in the face of scarcity,
so that the world will see we are faithful followers of Jesus,
who taught us to pray together:

The Lord's Prayer

Song

Closing responses:

Leader: Peace to the nations, east and west,
People: **peace to the nations, north and south.**

Leader: Peace to our neighbours, black and white,
People: **peace to our neighbours, young and old.**

Leader: Peace to all women, peace to all men,
People: **the peace of Christ above all peace.**

Appendix of resource material

Readings from the Revised Common Lectionary

Remembrance Sunday readings (UK) for Years A, B and C:

Year A

Joshua 24:1–3a, 14–25
with Psalm 78:1–7
Or Amos 5:18–24
with Psalm 70
1 Thessalonians 4:13–18
Matthew 25:1–13

Year B

Ruth 3:1–5, 4:13–17
with Psalm 127
Or 1 Kings 17:8–16
with Psalm 146
Hebrews 9:24–28
Mark 12:38–44

Year C

Isaiah 65:17–25
with Isaiah 12
Or Malachi 14:1–2a
with Psalm 98
2 Thessalonians 3:16–15
Luke 21:5–19

Song suggestions

The hymnals of many denominations often list appropriate hymns in their Subject Index under 'Remembrance Sunday' or 'National Occasions'. You will also find good song selections in a Subject Index under 'Justice' and 'Peace' themes. Following are some less common songs and hymns which offer texts appropriate for a Remembrance service. The authors of the texts are provided to help you find these songs in published resources.

'Christ be our Light', Bernadette Farrell

'Come now, O Prince of Peace', Geonyong Lee

'If the war goes on', John L Bell and Graham Maule

'Let there be light', Frances Wheeler Davis

'Lord, in this broken world', Kathleen Rowat

'Lord of life and Lord of nations', Anthony Kelly

'O day of peace', Carl P Daw

'Oh for a world …', Miriam Therese Winter

'The servant song', Richard Gillard

'To be a soldier', John L Bell and Graham Maule (based on words of George MacLeod)

'We lay our broken world', Anna Briggs

'Weary of all trumpeting', Martin H Franzmann

'What does the Lord require?' (many musical settings available of Micah 6:6–8)

'What shall we pray for those who died?', Carnwadric Parish Church (Glasgow) Worship Group

'When we are living, we are in the Lord', Roberto Escamilla, trans. John L Bell

Hands of remembrance: A symbolic action for children

– For this action, prepare a paper cutout of a hand, traced palm up with lines delineating the fingers, one for each child. You also need a pencil or a marker for each child.

– If your church has framed lists of members of the congregation who died in World War I and World War II, you could move those to a central location for this action. Or gather the children at a memorial plaque affixed to the wall.

Leader: The Prophet Isaiah once said to God's people, 'The Lord has comforted you, and will have compassion on all who suffer.'

But the people said, 'The Lord has forsaken us, God has forgotten us.'

The prophet answered the people, 'Can a woman forget her nursing child, or show no compassion to the child she's given birth to? I suppose even mothers may forget, but God will not forget you. Imagine, God has written your names on the palms of God's hands' (paraphrase of Isaiah 49:13b–16).

– Point out how hard it would be for a new mother to forget a baby she just gave birth to and is still nursing. That baby would cry, as babies do – so mothers can't forget them! Still, God remembers us even more than a nursing mother remembers her baby.

– Then point out how much easier it is to forget someone who lived a long time ago, someone we never knew. Even if they did something brave and honourable for us – like soldiers in World War I and World War II. If you have memorial plaques, read three or four names from the plaques as examples of people you never knew, and the children couldn't have known.

- Explain why it's important to remember people we never knew when they have done brave things for people *they* never knew – which is what we do on Remembrance Sunday.

- Isaiah's words are so important – God doesn't ever forget us. It's as if God has written each of our names on the palms of God's hands.

- Pass around the hand cutouts and give each child a pencil or marker. Invite them to write down a name, or many names, of people they want God to remember. If they know there was someone in their family who served in a war, invite them to include that name. If they aren't sure about names, invite them to write words like 'children who were afraid in wars' or 'soldiers who died saving a friend'. Give them a few examples of phrases in simple words.

- If you called the children forward, invite them to go back to their seats and to think about what they want to write. Tell them that their hands will become prayer hands later in the service.

- Either at the time of the Offering, or just before the Prayers for the World, arrange to collect the palms with names on them. Include the bidding for God to remember these names too. If there are very few names passed in, consider speaking them aloud. If there are many names, use a general bidding to include the names the children are remembering.

Notes:

1. From *Reason in Common Sense*, George Santayana, p.284 in Vol 1 The Life of Reason, 1905

2. Words from Aeschylus in 6th century BCE

Passages from NRSV copyright 1989, Division of Christian Education of the National Council of the Churches of Christ in the United States of America. Used by permission. All rights reserved.

Take three
An Advent or Christmas meditation on gifts and power

Stephen G Wright

Bible readings:

In the time of King Herod, after Jesus was born in Bethlehem of Judea, wise men from the East came to Jerusalem, asking, 'Where is the child who has been born king of the Jews? For we observed his star at its rising, and have come to pay him homage.'

(Matthew 2:1–2, NRSV)

On entering the house, they saw the child with Mary his mother, and they knelt down and paid him homage. Then, opening their treasure chests, they offered him gifts of gold, frankincense and myrrh.

(Matthew 2:11, NRSV)

Reflection:

Many Christmas carols and stories make mention of three kings who follow a star and come to pay homage to the baby Jesus in Bethlehem. In the Bible, they are not called kings, and their number is not specified; instead they are *'wise men from the East'*. In the centuries since, the magi have been interpreted as kings. Yet a magus, from which we get the word magician, was a sorcerer, shaman or priest: someone considered wise in lore, astrology, the healing arts and things beyond ordinary reality. Such persons were common all across the religious traditions of the Near and Middle East at the time.

The three gifts they bring were carefully chosen, not for their practical use, but for their many meanings, not least to do with different kinds of authority.

Gold signifies material wealth and power, but also untarnishable purity. Frankincense symbolises authority in religion, but also spiritual perfection. Myrrh represents the descent into death, but also authority over it. The three gifts represent key aspects of the authentic spiritual life, most especially aspects of power and how we approach it: whether it be used for worldly purposes, or in the service of the Beloved.

We see these three elements further drawn out at two key stages of Jesus' life in which he must make the right call, while others later make the wrong one.

When Jesus is tempted in the wilderness (Mt 4:1–11), in quick succession he is again offered three gifts. Depending on the choice he makes, these will either liberate him into a deeper path of service to the Presence, or draw him into the use of selfish, ego power and being a servant of the world of shadow.

The option to turn stones into bread to meet his craving for food suggests a temptation to self-satisfaction, rather than being satisfied with God.

Then bodily immortality and a chance to show his superiority over ordinary people is held out before him, as he is tempted to throw himself from the heights of the temple, knowing he will be preserved by angels.

Lastly, he is offered political power over all the kingdoms of the world …

Jesus rejects these temptations, recognising that the only power to which he must surrender is the Divine. Turning away from the dark forces that would entrap him, he passes through an initiation into the deep humility of the path of service: power under and with, rather than power over.

At the last, those three powers promised at birth, now integral to the very being of Jesus, are tested yet again when he is brought before three men, all of whom are diametrically opposed to the kind of authority embodied in those first 'three kings'.

Caiaphas is more interested in preserving religious orthodoxy and protecting his people from blasphemy (as he saw it) and the threat from Rome should Jesus' teachings inspire revolutionary fervour (Mt 26:57–68).

Before Herod, a man who is but a puppet king subject to Roman rule, Jesus is little more than a source of amusement to someone who, bereft of real authority, wants merely to be entertained and to bolster his own ego by belittling Jesus (Lk 23:6–12).

Lastly, Jesus comes before Pilate. This Roman governor's primary purpose is to secure the power of Rome against sedition. And he knows that if he does not do this, it will be his own head on the block. To quell any subversive activity, he takes the easy way out and offers the fate of Jesus to the mob (Lk 23:13–25).

All three of these men, like all of us, have choices to make about power and how to use it, choices about serving God or being self-serving, of love over fear. All three of these men chose to follow the I-me-mine path: power over others rather than power under and with.

Meditation:

If you have objects made of gold, and frankincense and myrrh, place them before you now, and/or light three candles to symbolise them.

Gold:

Where in your life have you preferred worldly power? ... At this point in your life, where does attachment to power still grip you? ... Do you need to feel that you must have authority over others or, come to that, yourself? ... Does the thought of not being in control of things frighten you? ... Are you inclined to want to keep a firm grip on everything, put the world to rights, stay in charge, rather than letting yourself be a pathway for the Beloved's Power and trusting that power to work in and through you? ...

Frankincense:

Do you see your connection to God, your spiritual life, as something you can 'get', if only you can do enough spiritual 'work' (whether it be Bible study or praying or whatever) rather than as a gift in your very being to which you need only wake up? ... Do you feel that to get to God you have to follow the rules, believe certain things, without which God will reject you, or send you to hell, or remain out of reach? ... Is spiritual awakening something you authentically desire, that you may become wiser and be of service to others, or something you want so that you have attained 'enlightenment', or self-gratification, or feel-good sentimentality to cope with the toughness of life, or as an insurance policy against damnation? ...

Myrrh:

Do you fear death and its aftermath? ... Fear aways teaches us something about the nature of our trust in the Beloved. For if we were completely trusting in the Divine, what happens after death would hold no fear for us. The Jesus story shows us power over death. Leaving aside theological arguments or doctrines about resurrection, is the idea of a life after death real and true to you, or something that you cling to in the hope that it is true and to keep the underlying fear of death at bay? ... Fear always shows us, among other things, where there is still a deepening of faith to be sought. Is your faith and relationship in the Beloved such that you *know* deeply that death is not the end? ...

The three gifts at Jesus' birth are not only signs of generosity from some of his first devotees, they are symbolic of three of the dominant themes of the spiritual life. They are not just for Christmas, but templates to be used throughout our lives as we walk the Way he showed us, as we follow the path that takes us away from the desire for worldly power and the attachments of the ego, and draws us into ever deepening humility, surrender and authenticity in the One in whom we live and move and have our being, and who lives and moves and has being in us.

Whenever we are offered the gifts and temptations of gold, frankincense and myrrh in our lives, may we prayerfully follow the Way that Jesus set for us.

In that lonely moment in the garden at Gethsemane, even he seems to waver, to want to live and not suffer the torture and death that awaited him. But he does what he always did: turns in trust to the Source of the power of life and prays, *'Yet not what I want, but what You want.'* (Mt 26:39, NRSV).

At Christmas, may we find the courage, in all that we face and will face in the future, to say, 'Thy will be done.'

Prayer:

May each of us be blessed
with the discernment
and strength
to know and follow that will.

Thy will be done.

Sources and acknowledgements

Passages from NRSV copyright 1989, Division of Christian Education of the National Council of the Churches of Christ in the United States of America. Used by permission. All rights reserved.

The light shines in the darkness
A service for Christmas Eve or for Christmas Day

Nancy Cocks

Introduction:

This is suitable for in-person worship or virtual delivery.

The scripture readings are taken from the NRSV.

If this service is used in daytime, be sure to edit the prayers to contrast day and night, dark and light, for the script was produced explicitly for Christmas Eve and an evening service.

Production notes and suggestions:

This service is designed around four monologues offered by symbols related to the Christmas narratives. These symbols can be represented by four objects (or by photos of these objects if you are producing a service delivered virtually): a lamp or candle on a stand, a wooden manger, a wooden staff or shepherd's crook, and a wrapped Christmas present.

If you are using photographs of the symbols for an online service, consider having a photo of the symbol on its own for the first section of the monologue and a photo of hands, or a person, engaging the symbol for the second section. For the final photo in the fourth monologue, create a tableau of all four symbols.

You need a minimum of three voices to lead the script well: a scripture reader, a monologue reader and a prayer leader, but it will be more effective if each monologue is delivered by a different voice.

A different reader could also be assigned for each scripture passage.

If you produce the script in a church sanctuary, each person who delivers a monologue can carry in the symbol and set it centrally. Create a tableau of the symbols that takes shape as the service unfolds.

The carols suggested are all very familiar. Anyone participating online will be able to sing along. Other songs which highlight the symbols or the different scenes of the narrative could be substituted.

The short prayers which follow the monologues were written to be said in unison. If this proves difficult for online participation, have a different voice lead those prayers, creating a little pause after each monologue. The longer prayer toward the end of the service has optional markings to add the sound of wind chimes or a bell as each theme of that prayer concludes. Instead, you could add a sung response or a short instrumental line from a carol at these places to draw listeners into the prayerful themes.

The Christmas story for the cosmos according to John:

In the beginning was the Word, and the Word was with God, and the Word was God. He was in the beginning with God. All things came into being through him, and without him not one thing came into being. What has come into being in him was life, and the life was the light of all people. The light shines in the darkness, and the darkness did not overcome it … And the Word became flesh and lived among us, and we have seen his glory, the glory as of a father's only son, full of grace and truth. *(Jn 1:1–5, 14)*

If it is your custom to light the Christ Candle on Christmas Eve, light it here.

(If the service is delivered virtually, invite those participating online to light a Christ Candle too.)

Carol: 'O come, all ye faithful'

'The lamp speaks' (The first monologue):

The light shines in the darkness and the darkness will not overcome it.
A lamp shines into the darkness, a pinpoint of light in a dark night.
We know how our eyes will find even the tiniest spark of light
when everything else around us is dark.
For light *is* stronger than the darkness.
At night, when a lamp is burning,
open the door on the darkness and see what happens.
The lamplight shines out and takes over a bit of the darkness.
Never does a piece of the darkness fall into a lighted room
and take away some of the light.

Even a simple lamp enjoys the power of light.
Its flame allows the light to shine where we need it –
into the darkest corners of house or stable.
A single lamp can show us the pathway on the darkest night,
so no one stumbles while carrying a precious gift.
A lamp shining in the doorway welcomes us in from our wandering.
Its warmth pushes away our worries
just like its light pushes away the dark.

The Christmas story according to Luke begins:

In those days a decree went out from Emperor Augustus that all the world should be registered. This was the first registration and was taken while Quirinius was governor of Syria. All went to their own towns to be registered. Joseph also went from the town of Nazareth in Galilee to Judea, to the city of David called Bethlehem, because he was descended from the house and family of David. He went to be registered with Mary, to whom he was engaged and who was expecting a child. *(Lk 2:1–5)*

Carol: 'O little town of Bethlehem'

'The lamp speaks again' (The first monologue continues):

But what is a lamp without hands to strike the match and light the wick?
A lamp cannot light itself.
What is a lamp without hands to hold it up
so its light shines into those dark corners?
A lamp cannot lift itself high.
What is a lamp without hands to open the door
and let the lamplight shine out into the darkness?
A lamp cannot open the door.

A lamp needs a life to look into the darkness
and see who needs light to brighten their path.
A lamp needs a life to light the wick and set the light shining.
A lamp needs a life to open the door and hold it up high,

a life that will welcome a stranger into the light, into the warmth,
into a heart and a hearth.

Prayer:

(Can be said in unison or led by a different voice)

O God, shine your light into our lives on this dark night. Warm our hearts so that we will open our doors to your love. May ours be the lives that shine light into the dark corners of your world. May ours be the lives that welcome you to be born again in our midst this Christmas. Amen.

'The manger speaks' (The second monologue):

What is a manger?
Just a few pieces of wood, nailed together, to serve a good purpose.
That's all a manger is.
Just a set of wooden arms,
strong enough to hold a new bundle of hay each day.
Still, a manger protects its bed of hay,
keeps it clean and dry, keeps the mice away.
A manger stands guard to offer its food, its source of life,
to animals who rely on its steady footing.
That manger always stands ready for whoever needs its nourishing cargo.
That manger will open its wooden arms
to welcome the hungry lives which gather round it,
lives that trust the manger holds what they need for the future.

The Christmas story according to Luke continues:

While they were there, the time came for her to deliver her child. And she gave birth to her firstborn son and wrapped him in bands of cloth, and laid him in a manger, because there was no place for them in the inn. *(Lk 2:6–7)*

Carol: 'Away in the manger'

'The manger speaks again' (The second monologue continues):

But how can a manger become a cradle for more than a bundle of hay?
Can it be a cradle without hands to prepare the bed and welcome more precious cargo?
Can a manger become a cradle without hands to lay a newborn to rest, hands which settle and sooth and tend new life?
Can a manger be a cradle without hands, tiny and perfect, reaching up, reaching out for attention, for warmth, for love?

A cradle needs a life to smooth the bed and smooth the forehead.
A cradle needs a life to rock the baby and sing the soothing lullaby.
A cradle needs a life to shelter, resting its tiny head, trusting itself to the manger's wooden arms and the mother's willing arms.

Prayer:

(Said in unison or led by a different voice)

O God, may our lives cradle your love this Christmas as we smile on the baby Jesus. May our love become a shelter for those who turn to us for protection. May our arms offer the welcome every stranger needs, in the name of Jesus who reaches out to us from the manger. Amen.

'The staff speaks' (The third monologue):

Not much goes into a staff.
It's cut from a tree and carved to be useful out there in the wild.
A staff is just a walking stick, sturdy and dependable,
something to lean on if you're weary.
A staff gives that extra footing when the path is slippery,
or your knee is stiff and sore, feeling the weather on a cold, damp night.
For a shepherd, a staff offers a bit of support along a rocky path.
That staff gives an occasional prod to remind a stubborn sheep
to move along to the next green pasture.
And a staff with a bit of a curve comes in handy
when a wayward lamb gets stuck in a crevice or a muddy patch in the field.

The Christmas story according to Luke continues:

In that region there were shepherds living in the fields, keeping watch over their flock by night. Then an angel of the Lord stood before them, and the glory of the Lord shone around them, and they were terrified. But the angel said to them, 'Do not be afraid; for see – I am bringing you good news of great joy for all the people: to you is born this day in the city of David a Saviour, who is the Messiah, the Lord. This will be a sign for you: you will find a child wrapped in bands of cloth and lying in a manger.' And suddenly there was with the angel a multitude of the heavenly host, praising God and saying,

> 'Glory to God in the highest heaven,
> and on earth peace among those whom God favours!'

When the angels had left them and gone into heaven, the shepherds said to one another, 'Let us go now to Bethlehem and see this thing that has taken place, which the Lord has made known to us.' So they went with haste and found Mary and Joseph, and the child lying in the manger. *(Lk 2:8–17)*

Carol: 'While shepherds watched their flocks'

'The staff speaks again' (The third monologue continues):

But what is a staff without hands to grip it firmly?
What is a staff without hands to place it wisely for sure support?
What is a staff without hands to prod that sheep
gently through the winding valley?
Hands to hook the crook around the silly lamb
that got stuck and pull it to safety?

A staff needs a life to test is strength.
A staff needs a life to lean on its dependability.
A staff needs a life who knows the sheep and sees how they go astray.
A staff needs a life unafraid of the danger,
a life to kneel down and rescue the lamb,
pulling it free, guiding it on the way.

Prayer:

(Said in unison or led by a different voice)

Lord Jesus Christ, we have come to find you this Christmas. Be our staff to lean on when we lose our footing. Be our guide when we cannot find our way. Pull us free from danger. Saviour, rescue us with the light of your love. Be our strength now and in the year ahead, so that we may walk with your courage and compassion, come what may. Amen.

If an offering is to be received, this is the place for it.

'A gift speaks' (The fourth monologue):

Christmas is a time of gift-giving.
Think of all the gifts wrapped up and waiting under your tree.
Each gift is a piece of love chosen for someone special.
Each gift is a piece of hope waiting to change someone's life.
A gift is that little piece of joy given to make someone smile.

The Christmas story according to Matthew:

In the time of King Herod, after Jesus was born in Bethlehem of Judea, wise men from the East came to Jerusalem, asking, 'Where is the child who has been born king of the Jews? For we observed his star at its rising, and have come to pay him homage.' … When they had heard the king, they set out; and there, ahead of them, went the star that they had seen at its rising, until it stopped over the place where the child was. When they saw that the star had stopped, they were overwhelmed with joy. On entering the house, they saw the child with Mary his mother; and they knelt down and paid him homage. Then, opening their treasure chests, they offered him gifts of gold, frankincense, and myrrh. *(Mt 2:1–2, 9–11)*

Carol: 'What child is this?'

'A gift speaks again' (The fourth monologue continues):

Yet what is a gift without hands to present it?
What is a gift without hands to unwrap it?
What is a gift without hands to hold it up in wonder,
to cherish it, to play with it,
to touch the love it bears and make that love your own?
A gift needs a life to give it.
A gift needs a life to receive it.
A gift needs a life to unwrap the love inside and share that love outside,
with all who wonder how love can give so much.

The Christ Child is a life born for us, born with us, to offer us God's gift.
The Christ Child is a gift, with love for each one of us so wonderful
that we can share that love with others and never have the love run out.
Christ is the gift God gives tonight.
Christ is the gift we receive tonight.
Unwrap this gift for yourself
and share this gift of love with everyone whose life touches yours.

Carol: 'Silent night'

Prayers of thanks and request:

God of the starry heavens and the good old earth,
Eternal God,
God with us,
you have come among us in the figure of a baby,
a newborn reaching out to us,
to bring a smile to our lips and hope to our hearts.
Thank you for your tenderness with which you touch our lives.

(Optional: Sound a chime or bell)

This Christmas, as we remember the baby lying in a manger,
we pray for peace …

Peace in all the places where there is anger or war or fear …
Peace in all the hearts that know sorrow or stress …
We pray for people who will not sleep safely tonight
because of conflict in their lives …

(Silence)

Cradle all these people and places in your love
so the world may sleep in heavenly peace this night.

(Optional: Sound a chime or bell)

This Christmas, as we remember the mother Mary rocking her baby,
we pray for all children born this Christmas season …
Watch over mothers and fathers and grandparents,
hoping for the best for their newborns …

(Silence)

Help us create communities where every child is valued
and every family has enough …
May families rejoice because Christ the Saviour is born for us,
for each of us and for all of us.

(Optional: Sound a chime or bell)

This Christmas, as we remember the father Joseph protecting his little one,
we pray for all those watching over the helpless
and the hopeless this season.

(Silence)

Be with all those who must work this holiday
to keep the world safe and to care for those in need …
Be with those who are sick or sad or lonely
so that each one will know your tender touch.

(Optional: Sound a chime or bell)

God of the starry heavens and the good old earth,
Eternal God, God with us,
this Christmas, as we remember the shepherds coming in haste
and the wise men coming in wonder,
open our hearts to reach out to the Christ Child,
to receive the gift you offer us in Jesus,
even as we offer our love to you in his name.
Bless us in the year ahead
so we can share your love with all the lives that touch ours.

(Optional: Sound a chime or bell)

May our hearts sing with the Christmas angels,
Glory to you, O God, and on earth, peace for all who wonder at your love.
Amen.

Carol: 'Joy to the world'

Blessing:

To you is born this day a Saviour who is Christ the Lord.
May the love of the Christ Child embrace you.
The joy of the Christ Child fill your heart.
May the peace of the Christ Child give you rest,
and the hope of the Christ Child guide you into the year ahead.
Amen.

Sources and acknowledgements

Passages from NRSV copyright 1989, Division of Christian Education of the National Council of the Churches of Christ in the United States of America. Used by permission. All rights reserved.

About the contributors

Rodney Aist is the Course Director at St George's College, Jerusalem, and is a pilgrimage scholar and Methodist pastor.

Alex Clare-Young is an Iona Community member and Co-Moderator of the Community's LGBTQ+ Common Concern Network. Alex is a minister in the United Reformed Church and a practical theologian, currently based in Cambridge City Centre. Alex's first book, *Transgender. Christian. Human.*, was published in 2019 by Wild Goose. They are a regular contributor to other Wild Goose books and resources. Their second book, *Trans Formation*, will be published by SCM Press in 2024.

Nancy Cocks is an associate member of the Iona Community and a retired minister and professor, who served as Deputy Warden on Iona in the early 2000s. She lives in Medicine Hat, Alberta where she is active in refugee settlement. She continues to produce worship resources and tries to pay more attention to her garden.

Ian M Fraser was one of the original members of the Iona Community. Throughout his life Ian travelled the world, most often with his beloved wife, Margaret, visiting basic Christian communities. He walked alongside slum dwellers in India and Haiti; Nicaraguan and Cuban revolutionaries; priests, nuns and catechists facing arrest and death in Central and South America; and small farming and fishing communities in the Philippines. Ian died in 2018, aged 100.

Kathy Galloway is an activist and writer. A member and former Leader of the Iona Community, she is the author of a dozen books on justice issues, spirituality and poetry. She lives in Glasgow.

Elaine Gisbourne is a member of the Iona Community, a palliative care physiotherapist with more than 17 years' experience working in hospices, and a spiritual director. She lives in North Yorkshire and enjoys tending the garden, walking her dogs in the beautiful landscape and practising contemplative prayer.

Rev. Dr Urzula Glienecke is a Latvian theologian, artist and activist living in Scotland. She is a member of the Iona Community and is currently working as one of the chaplains at the University of Edinburgh, collaborating with the Grassmarket Community Project, Cyrenians and others 'of all faiths and none'. She has worked, studied and taught in Latvia, Norway, Germany, Spain, the Republic of Ireland, Scotland and travelled around the world. She is passionate about working together with people on the margins and preserving our diverse and wonderful environment.

Tom Gordon has been a member of the Iona Community for 50 years. He was a parish minister in Edinburgh for 20 years and chaplain at the Marie Curie Hospice for 15 years. A regular contributor to Wild Goose Publications, his books cover hospice chaplaincy, loss, grief and bereavement, contemporary parables and daily readings. He also offers a 'Thought for the day' in a daily blog: see https://swallowsnestnet.wordpress.com. He is married to Mary, has three children, two grandsons and a mad cocker spaniel.

John Harvey: Molly and I have found ourselves sharing much of our lives with families and individuals living in poverty over the decades – a privilege, we have deeply believed, for people like ourselves from very comfortable backgrounds. In particular, as well as both being part of the Gorbals Group ministry in the 1960s, Molly served as Coordinator of a charity working alongside people living in poverty for 15 years, and I served three church parishes in areas of deprivation. Twelve or so years ago, we were part of the group who began the Poverty Truth Commission movement here in Glasgow, which has now spread throughout the UK – we still remain connected. Now long retired, we remain in personal touch with a number of the individuals and families we have travelled with over the years. The royalties from the liturgy *Remember Me* will be donated to the Poverty Truth Commission.

Janet Lees is a member of the Lay Community of St Benedict and a former school chaplain. Other examples of her work using the Remembered Bible are published by Wild Goose.

John Murning has served in the Parishes of New Cathcart, United Church of Bute, Denny Old, and Sherwood Greenlaw in Paisley and had a short spell as an Army chaplain. He has also served on a part-time basis as a hospital, industrial and football club chaplain. He has been involved with Spill the Beans, an Internet all-age worship resource with a Scottish flavour, and is a contributor to various Wild Goose books.

The Rev'd Sr Sandra Sears CSBC is a Local Priest in the Anglican Diocese of Willochra in rural South Australia, and a member of the Community of Sts Barnabas and Cecilia. As well as poetry, stories and liturgical resources she is a composer of songs and hymns suitable for congregational use, especially those in country areas with minimal musical resources.

Thom M Shuman, an Iona Community associate member living in Columbus, Ohio, is a frequent contributor to Wild Goose anthologies, downloads and books. A retired Presbyterian minister, he serves a church part-time and writes every day.

Jan Sutch Pickard is a poet, storyteller and former Iona Abbey Warden who lives on the Isle of Mull.

Kira Taylor is a journalist and writer who focuses on energy, climate and environment issues.

Simon Taylor is a Baptist minister in Exeter and the Free Church Chaplain at the University of Exeter. He enjoys writing prayers and liturgies for everyday use and special occasions. These often draw on images from nature and especially Dartmoor where he likes to walk.

Bob Warwicker is a retired minister of the United Reformed Church. The Good Friday liturgy originated in Huddersfield, where Christians have come together on Good Friday for over 70 years to worship on a hill overlooking the town.

Iain Whyte has been a member of the Iona Community since 1966. He is a retired minister of the Church of Scotland, was University Chaplain in St Andrews and Edinburgh, and Head of Christian Aid Scotland for four years. Iain has been a longstanding human rights activist with experience of West and Southern Africa, and recently has researched and written on historical and modern slavery and the abolition movement. He is a Trustee for STEPS (St Andrews Education for Palestinian Students).

Isabel Whyte was a member of the Iona Community, a teacher, a Church of Scotland minister and a Health Care Chaplain with involvement in justice and peace initiatives in the UK and overseas, and was involved in conflict transformation as a mediator for Place for Hope. Isabel shared with Iain in promoting international friendship and hospitality and many tributes for this were received after Isabel died in April 2022.

Stephen G Wright has spent many decades exploring spirituality, specifically, because of his academic and nursing background, in relation to health. He is a member of the Iona Community and the Anglican Church, and a teacher of the contemplative Way. A poet and pilgrim, his latest book with Wild Goose, *The Kentigern Way*, focuses on the life of Kentigern/Mungo and offers a pilgrimage route around the Northern Fells of Cumbria. His other books include *Coming Home, Contemplation, Burnout* and *Heartfullness*. The last of these is the culmination of 20 years of work and the teachings offered in the Kentigern School for Contemplatives. Stephen is a Fellow and visiting professor at the University of Cumbria. At 73 he still finds working as a trustee and spiritual director for the Sacred Space Foundation a joy: www.sacredspace.org.uk

Wild Goose Publications, the publishing house of the Iona Community established in the Celtic Christian tradition of Saint Columba, produces books, e-books, CDs and digital downloads on:

- holistic spirituality
- social justice
- political and peace issues
- healing
- innovative approaches to worship
- song in worship, including the work of the Wild Goose Resource Group
- material for meditation and reflection

Visit our website at
www.ionabooks.com
for details of all our products and online sales